INTERIOR DESIGN CLIENTS

THE DESIGNER'S GUIDE TO BUILDING AND KEEPING A GREAT CLIENTELE

BY THOMAS L. WILLIAMS

D0054807

ALLWORTH PRESS
NEW YORK

To Robert,
For supporting me in everything I do

14   13   12   11   10   5   4   3   2   1

Published by Allworth Press
An imprint of Allworth Communications
10 East 23rd Street, New York, NY 10010

Cover design by Kristina Critchlow
Interior design by Kristina Critchlow

Page composition/typography by Integra Software Services, Pvt., Ltd., Pondicherry, India

ISBN: 978-1-58115-676-8

Library of Congress Cataloging-in-Publication Data:
Williams, Thomas L., 1949–
    Interior design clients : the designer's guide to building and keeping a great clientele / by Thomas L. Williams.
        p. cm.
Includes index.
ISBN 978-1-58115-676-8 (pbk. : alk. paper)
1. Interior decoration—Marketing.
2. Customer relations.
I. Title.   II. Title: Designer's guide to building and keeping a great clientele.
    NK2116.2.W56 2010
    747.068—dc22   2010008022

Printed in Canada

CONTENTS

Keep love in your heart. A life without it is like a sunless garden when the flowers are dead.

– Oscar Wilde

FOREWORD

One of my earliest memories of explaining my mother's profession was correcting those much older than I. "Oh, that's so nice that your mother is an interior decorator," they would proclaim. I was always strangely annoyed and exclaimed, "She's not a decorator, she's an interior designer." At the time, I did not know about the list of differences, but I knew my mother was a businesswoman first and an interior designer second.

As businesspeople first, we are empowered to be the creative geniuses that we were blessed to be. Without business prowess and sense, there are no clients to design for and there is no money to design with. It is no coincidence that many great artists only realized their full fame posthumously—after a businessperson successfully marketed and sold the fated artists' works at their true values. As those who studied the great artists also know, many of these creative divas were unable to work well with others, rendering them completely useless in any client interactions. We do not want to be one of those divas.

We must be people-people. Often it seems that, in addition to countless other hats, interior designers must be armchair psychologists—assuaging clients' fears and anticipating clients' moves before they know the moves themselves. To be a good businessperson, it is not necessary to treat your clients like boardroom adversaries, but rather to take the finesse that you apply to each lovely room and to carefully cultivate and massage each client relationship to keep them and their friends coming back for more.

I was fortunate enough to meet Tom at, what else, a conference about the business of interior design. Immediately, one could see the grace and respect with which Tom approached his business, as it is equal to the grace and respect with which Tom approaches others. His communication style is impeccable and his self-presentation thoughtful.

As a follow up to Tom's first book, *Starting Your Career as an Interior Designer*, this book more closely examines the lifeblood of our firms—the client. In this book, he lets us, as the readers, get inside his head and carefully examine the gray matter that makes this interior designer/businessman/gentleman successful. The mixture of anecdotes, teachings, and case studies ensure that this book reads less like a dreaded textbook and more like a novel.

Most importantly, Tom begins the book with the first chapter on the "Ideal Client"—our foundation. It is not the client who is perfectly happy that you go to sleep worrying over and wake up thinking about, but rather the client that you knew was not the right fit for your firm, yet you decided to take on anyway. These are not bad people, but they are bad clients for you. Learning to identify and work with not only your *good* clients, but also your *ideal* clients will bring you great success.

We work in a fragmented industry. In fact, according to recent U.S. Census reports, most interior designers work for a firm of four or fewer. Chances are, if you are reading this book you are the head honcho of a firm of four or fewer. Chances also are that, as business owner and designer extraordinaire, you are not only tasked with being a creative director of your firm but also with ensuring that the clients are appropriately cared for, that the books are in good shape, that you are networking with the right people and in the right places, that you are up to speed on industry news and technologies, and responsible for a myriad of other tasks that keep you working late into the night.

We are in a client-centric industry. Without thinking of the client or the potential client at each step of the way, our firms suffer and under-perform. Tom walks through each client interaction and eloquently describes, often times through case studies, the best practices for gracefully and appropriately working with clients to achieve our penultimate goal—a successful project and, more importantly, a successful relationship that stands the test of time.

Without clients, we have no business. Without business, we have no meaningful creative outlet.

Alexandra C. Gibson
CEO, Gibson Design Management
Managing Partner, Gibson Design Group
Charlottesville, Virginia

INTRODUCTION

In the world of professional interior design, clients reign supreme. Their every want and need is met and supplied by professional designers all over the country and the world. These clients can be demanding and particular about their selections and persnickety and tedious with observations about recently delivered products. They can also be delightfully inspiring and wonderfully receptive to the process of creation and implementation. The choice of how to proceed is up to you, the designer. It is you, after all, who must orchestrate and manage every aspect of this competitive and complex production we call interior design. There are a few questions you might ask to clarify what is needed to succeed.

When you work with your clientele, are you as pleased with the results as you should be and do they continue to come back to you for assistance? Do you find it difficult to create a marketing campaign designed to bring in the high-profit clientele other designers in your area seem to find everywhere they turn? Does it seem as if presentations become bogged down in minutia and last minute changes that you and your staff find difficult to control? Do orders become a behind-the-scenes nightmare for all concerned, and do you find deliveries are late or damaged in shipment? Are there times when you feel as if you have too many staff and other times when there just aren't enough hands to go around? In short, do you feel as if you don't have any real control over clients and the decisions they need to make to get a project off the ground and completed in a timely and efficient manner? Well, you're not alone. How, you ask, is it possible to manage your client, their project, your business, and the multitude of tasks necessary to bring an interior design project to fruition? You see your peers out there working with clients all the time with smiles on their faces, skipping through the world of client and project management. Their clients seem to hang onto every word uttered and the collaboration appears to be made in heaven. What do these designers do to make it so easy, and why can't you have the same type of client? Actually, you can.

Clients, first of all, are not some abstract entity from another planet, though you might think otherwise from time to time. Not only are they your bread and butter, but they are also individuals with personalities, needs, and desires. Your understanding of how they tick is a vital part of finding, working with, and keeping them as customers of your services. Your focused and professional regard for their requirements in the field of interior design is what will bring them to you time and time again.

Would it surprise you to know that many of these very same clients started out fearful of the design process? Yes, fearful. They feel almost naked in your presence. How, you ask, is that possible? You are, after all, sensitive to their needs and knowledgeable about the process of interior design. Most professional interior designers don't start out by trying to intimidate their clients, do they? On occasion, that might happen, but you're not one of them, are you? I hope not, because client and project management requires you to leave your ego at the door and focus on clients and their expectations. So why, exactly, are clients fearful of working with interior designers? There are a number of reasons why clients dread designers coming into their homes.

First, and foremost, clients worry you will judge what they have done prior to calling you. What was done in the past and by whom doesn't matter; they will think it doesn't live up to your standards. That is, after all, why they decided to call you, isn't it? This, of course, gives you a wonderful advantage but don't be tempted to use it for any short-term gain. Remember, you're in this for the long haul, so don't be too quick to judge.

Second, clients are terrified that you will spend far more money than they have budgeted for the project. Most, if not all, have no real understanding of the budget creation and management process. Professional interior designers should be adept at eliciting pertinent information to use in budget preparation. It will be your job to organize all the disparate parts of the project to arrive at a realistic and manageable budget. You must also educate your clients to help them understand the choices each of you is about to make and how a well-grounded budget will be an essential part of the process.

Third, clients are embarrassed to admit they don't necessarily know all the terms you will use while creating the project. Many of them are overwhelmed by terms we professionals roll off our tongues with ease. An important part of our ability to manage clients is to use words and phrases that are recognized and understood by all concerned. Your ability to use the correct term and make sure clients understand the meaning will help alleviate their fears and, at the same time, ensure your meaning is never misconstrued.

Fourth, clients obsess over making the correct decision. Thorough preparation and presentation of your design schemes will help your clients arrive at the proper choice for their interiors. At the same time you will be showing them the best possible selections for the project upon which you are working. Your professional approach to the creation of interiors and calm presentation of choices will help your clients develop trust in you and your design decisions. As they become more comfortable with your ability to define their needs, it will be apparent you are focused on offering them satisfying choices that will enhance the project.

Finally, clients are afraid they will have no say in what the space will look like. Your ability to ask the right questions and come up with the best possible solutions is part and parcel of professional client and project management. Your acumen in interpreting the client's input is essential to the satisfactory completion of any project. It's your job to understand how clients will use the space and whether or not their likes and dislikes are addressed. It's their home, not yours.

In the pages that follow you will be introduced to an array of professional interior designers from across the country. Each has contributed his or her thoughts and ideas on how best to manage clients and projects to a successful conclusion. These case studies are invaluable in the study of how to maintain clients in the competitive world of interior design. With the help of these dedicated professionals, we'll explore the steps you will take to define, market to, and acquire your optimum clients. These design colleagues will also help you understand how to prepare and deliver presentations designed to help your clients visualize their space as never before. With the help of other professionals from varied segments of the interior design industry, we will manage the maze of product procurement, delivery, and after-sales satisfaction.

As a professional interior designer you must allay your client's fears and create a project that is exciting, fun, and devoid of judgmental observations. The steps taken to ensure a seemingly seamless process are the heart and sole of client and project management—not as easy as it sounds when clients are in the throes of worry and doubt. The easygoing designers you see at the markets all the time have worked long and hard to create a supportive environment for their clients and make it easy for them to move the project forward. They have studied who their best clients are and spent hours creating the right environment to nurture them. They have honed their creative and presentation skills and have infrastructure within their firms to support project management and product delivery. They spend time with clients after the project is finished to ascertain exactly what went right and what could be improved. In short, they are professionals in a sea of mediocrity. Without a clear understanding of what makes a client tick you will never succeed. Although creating lovely interiors is what brought most of us to the field, client and project management sustains a business and separates the professionals from the wannabes.

CHAPTER ONE

THE IDEAL CLIENT

> "One's first love is always perfect until one meets one's second love."
>
> — Elizabeth Aston, *The Exploits & Adventures of Miss Alethea Darcy,* 2005

It's easy to imagine that all you have to do to bring oodles of clients to your door is be a great interior designer with wonderful taste. Think again. Attracting clients requires a whole lot more than a shiny new interior design degree from your local university. Just because you passed the NCIDQ (National Council for Interior Design Qualification) test doesn't necessarily mean you have a clue about finding and keeping great clients. There is so much more to client management that simply isn't taught in design school. You may think you're qualified, but without a clear understanding of the myriad tools needed to create and manage clients and projects, you won't succeed. The nice thing about these tools is they can be learned. Once you decide to apply the lessons to the challenge the rest will become a cakewalk.

You should have defined the type of interior design you want to practice and who your clientele will be as part of your overall business plan. If not, now is the time to organize your thoughts and decide just what type of client you prefer to work with. This question is important when you set out on the initial interview to start a new project. Client management includes understanding who will be a good fit for your firm and a profitable addition to your bottom line. As a business owner, it is up to you to define your market.

It's Not a Popularity Contest

So many variables go into determining who your best and most profitable client might be. Start by asking yourself what type of person you find easiest to work with. Do you enjoy the level-headed attorney type who will make a decision after a complete review of the details? What about the stay-at-home mom who must see every fabric available before making a choice? How about the couple who can't agree on what color they want in the family room? These types, and more, are the clients of today. Most often, you will work with couples, and one will usually be the spokesperson. Make sure you define him or her early on. After all, you want decisions to be made in a timely manner. It's also important for your clients to understand that they both can't try to give you direction then use you as the go-between in disputes about the choices that will need to be made. Projects need to move forward to be profitable. You also do not want to be put in the position of family counselor. Once you've defined the types of clients you enjoy working with, you need to ask yourself a few more questions. Is that person or couple able to give you business on a regular basis, and will they spend enough with your firm to make them worthwhile? Will there be enough profit in each transaction to maintain the overhead you've created for your business? If you have employees, will this client help keep them productive? The point, of course, is to ensure that you and your business create the most beautiful and appropriate space for the client while making money.

It's Not Always About the Money

As part of your business plan, you have ascertained where you expect to find business and who will be bringing that business to your firm. Not every client needs to be Mr. and Mrs. Warbucks. As a matter of fact, most interior design firms in America work with clients who earn less than $200,000 a year. Does that surprise you? It shouldn't. Although the large firms with flashy names garner a huge amount of press, far more is spent with smaller firms on projects that will never be presented by *Architectural Digest.* That is not a bad thing. It represents an opportunity for you to find steady work and earn a good living. The type of clients with whom you work and the amount they spend will change as you gain experience and grow as a designer and business person. Early in your career it might make more sense to focus on what some refer to as the "low-hanging fruit." By that I mean those clients who are more readily available to designers who don't have the prestigious credentials and experience needed to attract more affluent customers. That's not to say you shouldn't strive for larger jobs and more important clients; they may come as you mature in your career. That, too, should be part of your business plan. More established designers often work with more demanding clients who require, and are willing to pay for, the skills and resources of an experienced business professional. Successful designers attract this type of client with accomplished marketing campaigns and through great word of mouth created over a period of time.

Where Did All These People Come From?

Depending on where in the country you live, your clients most often will work as senior executives, or they will be doctors, lawyers, or real estate tycoons. Some may own their own businesses. You shouldn't be surprised; that's where the money is. Entrepreneurs and small businesses make up the bulk of business in the United States and account for more employment than almost all the larger corporations in this country. And yes, you will be looking for clients who have the disposable income needed for most interior design projects. These clients will also probably be somewhere between thirty-five and sixty years old. Old enough for the kids to be in college or just graduated. They will have been homeowners for a decade or two and might even own a second home or time-share. Retirement income and IRAs have been established and enough cash is available for day-to-day living. A lot of the expenses of youth are long past and the focus has now become more about style and substance. Hence, extra money for interior design.

Clients in their twenties and thirties are far more Internet savvy, have smaller budgets, and will "shop" the interior designer if given the chance. Young homeowners, generally, are still focused on creating a home for themselves and the kids and saving for future college tuition. Clothing, food, and the essentials of living are all part of younger couples' challenges. Once that hurdle is cleared they are ready for you. This market, however, shouldn't be ignored. As with all generalities there will be exceptions. If you are more comfortable working with people in this age and demographic group, then by all means nurture that relationship. These clients will someday grow into prime clients with disposable income.

If you, too, are in your twenties or thirties and would like to have a clientele that grows with you, this is your group. You might find it easier to educate them in the ways of professional interior design, and they will become very comfortable working within your parameters. Most designers, however, look for a mix of clientele for the variety and challenge each brings to the table.

Smaller Percentages, Bigger Profits

These clients will further divide into two groups. Twenty percent of these clients will give you 80 percent of your business. Known as Pareto's Law, or the 80:20 Rule, this axiom will remain true throughout your career. The 80:20 Rule applies in almost every sphere. You noticed it in school. You found it on your first job. In almost any business, 20 percent of the resource, or production, will produce 80 percent of the results. You should also understand the reverse is true. A project, or work, that takes up 80 percent of your time will produce only 20 percent of your profit. Only after completing a few jobs will you be able to look at profits and see who, of your clientele, falls into the positive side of the 80:20 Rule. You will find these clients easiest to work with and manage, and they will continue to come back for more work. They will also be the ones who refer you to their friends and colleagues. As you continue your practice, you will take on many new clients—all of whom will fall into the 80:20 categories. The 80 percent are the ones to evaluate on a regular basis. Some, if managed properly, may move into the 20 percent group but, generally, they will stay in the 80 percent group. At some point you may decide to cut ties with those clients and move on. That will be up to you. It is, after all, your business.

Tanya Shively, ASID, of Sesshu Design Associates, Ltd., in Scottsdale, Arizona, has been practicing interior design in her area for a number of years, and her perspective as to who her optimum client is makes for a great case study.

"In identifying your ideal client it is important to examine three areas—first, yourself and your passion, second, your typical clients' demographics (where they live, how much they earn, and who they are), and third, their psychographics—what they want and how they make their buying decisions.

On the Inside Looking Out

You may be surprised to hear that to discover your ideal client, you must first look at yourself. Understanding yourself and your passions is the key to finding people with whom you will enjoy spending a lot of time. You should consider what types of design you like best and whether there is a particular style or aspect that most interests you. Do you love French Country, or is the kitchen the area you enjoy digging into for clients? You may discover you particularly enjoy the resort style of mountain homes design and would like to focus on that clientele.

Once you have your specialty narrowed down, think about your personality, how you get along with other people, and the types of clients with whom you work best. For instance, do you enjoy clients who want to be heavily involved in every aspect and just need you to guide them, or do you prefer to create a concept yourself and present the whole thing in one big, fantastic, blow-their-socks-off presentation? Are you good at remaining calm under high pressure, or do you prefer to be more laid back and take things as they come?

Defining how you prefer to operate and the personality types you get along with easily will help clarify the clients who will make your work life enjoyable, rather than stressful. Who are these people and where do you find them?

Come Out, Come Out, Wherever You Are!

Once you have a clear picture of your work process and the type of clients with whom you like to work, you can begin to think about where to find them. A good place to start is with your existing or previous clients. Who did you most enjoy working with, and what are their general characteristics? Are they married or single, male or female? How old are they? What type of work do they do? Where do they live, and what is their net worth or income level? Most likely you will begin to see a pattern emerge, which is known as the demographic profile of your ideal client.

The demographic profile, however, may still be too broad for an effective marketing strategy. This is where determining the psychographic profile of your client will help. Within that large group of people who fit your ideal client description, there will be subgroups centered around interests. Understanding your personal passion and combining it with the psychology of your optimum client will help define where you will search for clients. If, for instance, you love creating French Country style kitchens, you can search for other markets those clients frequent, which might include art galleries, antique shops, wine stores, and food emporiums. What other things would people who love that style kitchen like? Where do they shop? What do they read? By understanding what their interests are, you begin to know where you might search for them and how they make their buying decisions. Are they on the Internet, or are they less likely to embrace technology, making Internet advertising a waste of time and money? Certain interests may also further refine the age and gender profile. People who love French Country may tend to be older, predominately single females.

It's Not Extra Sensory Perception

Once you have defined your ideal client profile and understand who they are and what they like, you can move on to creating your USP—Unique Selling Proposition. Your USP helps to illustrate who you are and what you do to exactly the right people—your potential clients. It is a way of clarifying and distilling down to a single short sentence exactly what you do and what makes you different from other designers. It answers the question, "Why should we work with you?" It helps to determine the clients who will be happiest with your services and leaves out those who will be difficult and time consuming for you. This goes hand in hand with the 80:20 rule, which states that 20 percent of your clients will bring you 80 percent of your profits and business. Those 20 percent are your ideal clients. With the right USP, you will automatically and easily reach more of those who are like the 20 percent you love to work with. It is the key to understanding your optimum client and creating your marketing message."

Client Management Is All About Teaching

Some of your most interesting and profitable clients will be those who look to you for guidance and education. You may find your responsibilities, as a professional designer, will also include being a teacher. After all, you have the experience to define what is best in most design situations. You will need to make sure your clients understand everything you present and are in tune with your sense of style and what is needed to move the project forward. You should never talk down to these clients. After all, they are paying for your expertise in interior design, so you will want to explain each of your choices in a clear and straightforward manner. Listening to clients is also very important. Take the time to let them know you hear what they are saying. That may mean keeping your mouth shut from time to time. Don't be in a hurry to answer each and every statement they might make with a rebuttal of your own. Be secure in your choices and be prepared to explain in very professional and complete detail why the choice made is the best for a particular situation. This part of the equation requires you to be versed in all areas of interior design. You will want to live and breathe design every day. Your continuing education ensures your clients will feel secure in your choices for them, and you will feel secure in the knowledge that you have presented the best possible solution for the project.

Kathryn Long, ASID, of Ambiance Interiors in Asheville, North Carolina works in an area of historic importance that also has a large resort containing a number of second homes. She works in new construction, renovation, and historic preservation.

"I often meet people in social situations, like a cocktail party, who, when they discover I am a professional interior designer, react in one of two ways. Chatterbox number one says, 'Oh, you're an interior designer (although they usually change 'designer' to 'decorator'); that must be such *fun!*' Guest number two opines, 'Oh, wouldn't you just love to have a client with an unlimited budget who just turns the project over to you to do anything you wish?' Each, of course, is unaware of the time, dedication, and education required to become a professional interior designer.

So many people share the opinion of chatterbox number one that I usually just smile and move on. It's guest number two I find more interesting. I begin by explaining how much more rewarding I find working with clients to achieve their dream home environments using whatever budget they have rather than a 'the sky is the limit–do what you want' approach.

Comfort Is Key

Ideal clients are those who have at least some idea of the visual direction they want for their home. If they haven't considered visual direction they should be honest and let the designer help them determine what they want. Almost everybody says 'comfortable.'

The next step is to help the clients define what that means to them. A client who has already given thought to this and who has books and magazines with pages marked to show me what comfort and relaxed chic means to them can get a project started more quickly. It is essential to have that definition before starting the project.

All of this is part of the ongoing importance of communication, and it must continue throughout the project to keep your optimum client engaged and happy. Optimum clients are also honest and good listeners who are respectful of you, your talent, and your time. These clients tend to consistently respond in a timely manner to e-mails, voicemails, and any other type of message. They know their budget and will work to stay within the parameters set by each of you. I have found men and women who have been employed often make excellent clients. These clients have a better understanding of how we professional interior designers operate and how important our contribution is to the project. Also, and this may seem contrary to that, I have found that clients with 'old money' are more appreciative of my work and are more comfortable spending their money than 'nouveau riche' clients. I have not found that people in any particular profession make good or bad clients. Attorneys can be very analytical, but that is not always a negative thing.

The Importance of Communication

I prefer working with a couple versus working only with the wife who is then charged with communicating to her husband (after he gets home from a long day at the office) my ideas and summarizing our meeting. Quite often men are not enthusiastic about change, and it is important that a couple be on the same page before beginning. Optimum clients understand this and work with the interior designer to communicate ideas and maintain trust.

I often have clients building second homes, and the husband is always more involved. I think because the home is not the primary residence, both clients are more relaxed about choices and want to make their second home very different from their main domicile. Both probably have a love of the area and have vacationed here before. It creates a more relaxed atmosphere. When the couple comes into my office/design studio they make decisions much more rapidly and we move forward with the project in a timely manner.

Don't forget repeat clients as optimum clientele. The easiest, most fun-filled, and most efficient projects are with repeat clients. You already know and trust each other. Repeat clients know how you work, what decisions they will need to make, and when they must make them. They are prepared for the process and generally come to the first meeting with a wealth of ideas for the new project. I always maintain contact with past clients to make sure they think of my firm when considering a new design plan."

It's My Party

From the very beginning it is important that your clients understand and recognize how your firm operates. You will have presented a letter of agreement or contract outlining the scope of services. The client will have signed it and given you a retainer for your design time or fees. Never allow the client to define how you will do business. For you to perform as a professional designer and manage your clients, you must remain in charge of the process.

Clients should also recognize your position as a professional. Long shopping days together with lunches at the design center don't define your position as the CEO of your design firm. You should be comfortable with your client, and in many instances you may be on a first name basis. That does not mean you are friends. These people are your clients first, and as such should be shown the respect due them. They, too, should show you the respect you deserve as a professional. Never blur the line between client and social acquaintance. Dinner in their home, outings with the kids, or weekends at their country place should be out of bounds. You have a job to do, and it requires you to keep a professional distance in order to perform to the best of your ability. Well-managed clients understand the distinction and will abide by your rules.

Once the project is completed, you might decide to invite the couple to lunch to discuss how they feel the project went and whether or not there are areas in which your firm might improve. You might also ask if the couple would allow you to host a large cocktail party or afternoon affair to show off the new space. They would then become spokespeople for your firm and help with its success.

Keep in mind that well-managed clients will pay invoices on time and will understand your position as a small business owner. Cash flow is important, and, although you won't discuss this particular part of your business with your clients, most will understand the need for timely payments. It's also important you are vigilant about precise proposals, invoices, and design fee charges. A mistake on any of these statements will last a long time in the memory of most clients. You will lose a certain amount of trust, and it will be very hard to regain the stature you had in the beginning.

From the Client's Perspective

Thus far, I have focused on what traits the interior designer should be looking for in optimum clients, which is an important part of client and project management. We should not, however, completely ignore clients' desires. They will be coming to you with a certain set of ideas about how the project might move forward. Defining management within the context of interior design while being mindful of what the client expects from the process is an important part of your job. As you will see in chapter three, listening and understanding what the client has to say about the project is important to successful client management. Having a clear understanding of their expectations and how they came to your design firm will help you create a calm and efficient client and project management style. I think it would be instructive and enlightening, now, to hear what a client has to say about the optimum interior designer.

Mrs. Norma Carney is classified by our firm as an optimum client. My partner, Robert, and I have worked with Mrs. Carney for a number of years. Norma is a retired computer scientist, an equestrian, a portfolio manager, and an aspiring botanist. She likes classical music, opera, math, physics, Tibetan Buddhism, and economics. She owns two Dobermans and six rescue cats, all of whom live in her house. With this wonderful range of interests, Norma's focus on the interior design of her home is part of a very rich and interesting life. Here are a few of her observations.

Know What You Want

"After spending some years pursuing just the right look and feel, inside and out, for my home, I have realized it was and is my mother's home that I want. Not her actual home, but the image of her home as it lives in my memory. I cherish that. I am not one of those women who live to rebel against their mothers' tastes. My mother died when I was a child, and it has been a lifelong goal to recreate her presence in my life. This search is reflected in the design elements I love: Rooms that look like the insides of jewel boxes, filled with polished wood floors and furniture, deeply-colored silks, fine china, and an overall theme of classical grace and beauty. The personal and fundamental ideas that drive your taste in design need to be communicated to the professionals with whom you work, even if you think your reasons are logically indefensible.

When to Say No

As a client, I could tell you some stories about designers behaving badly right inside my home. Initially, while looking for an interior design professional to redo my modest 1950s ranch home, I interviewed several local women designers whose names I found in the phone book. The first designer showed up at my home with a picture book filled with hotel room interiors that featured those big, boxy, neutral-toned stuffed chairs, facing an equally neutral (i.e. bland) table, surrounded by pastel doodads and forgettable floor lamps. She was very proud of her hotel work and felt it honestly revealed her acumen as a residential interior designer. When I showed her my kitchen, the wallpaper, flooring, and tiles of which I had selected some years before, she burst out, 'Oh my God! Who did *this*?' as if she had encountered old goat heads nailed to the walls. I felt it somewhat important to rise to the occasion, so I answered, bravely, 'I did.' She was, however, unstoppable. She was on a mission. She bulldozed her way through the rest of the house, telling me how everything in sight would 'have to go,' presumably to be replaced with pastel hotel units. She clearly felt sorry for me for living in such conditions of aesthetic squalor. I never called her back.

The next woman showed up at my house with an almost identical book of project pictures. She was just as adamant that I let her take over for me. I started to wonder if all the designers south of San Francisco had the same hotel room pictures in their portfolios, and if they all felt they should be allowed to dictate the interiors of my home. There are many designers who are only too willing to impose their vision of 'good taste' on the client, with the result being a happy designer but an unhappy client. Clients should recognize their homes as personal temples. When it comes to interior designers, there are some who will be trespassers. Show them to the door.

Finding a Match

After several years of reading every issue of *Architectural Digest* and *Traditional Home* and several months of searching, I met Thomas completely by chance inside the main hall of a local mall. He and his partner, Robert, were putting on an informational presentation about the work that they do as interior designers, which included tables of project photos and supplier samples. By this time, I had a very good sense of what kind of interiors I wanted and what types of furniture and materials I wanted to use. As I lingered around the tables, I noticed that many of the samples were from my favorite lines and that many of the photos showed finished rooms that really appealed to me. When I realized that Thomas and Robert were local, I made an appointment to meet them in their showroom.

Working with Your Designer

The first meeting went well, not because of any elaborate presentations, sales pitches, or attempts to impose a style on me, but because I sensed Robert and Thomas could and would create a set of home interiors that would make my dreams of recreating my mother's house come true. As our working relationship progressed, they never questioned my taste, and they always offered many thoughtful choices of colors, fabrics, and furnishings. They never minded when I said no; they simply created what I wanted. Robert and Thomas scanned many, many pages of the magazine pictures I had spent months tearing out and grouping. I used the pictures to help explain my vision and help them achieve it. Their work blended so seamlessly with my idea of the perfect home that it never occurred to me that their own personal tastes were any different from my own.

The Remodel Team

In addition to creating the interior of my home, Robert and Thomas introduced me to a necessary element in a structural remodel: the design/build team. I had decided to expand my home and simply didn't know how to proceed. It probably would have taken me months of searching and interviewing to find someone to build anything I might have designed. Robert and Thomas' recommendation of a local design/build firm with whom they had worked before turned out to be a perfect match. Not only did the designers, as project managers, work beautifully with the builders, the entire team went out of their way to make the experience as painless as possible for me. There were no construction horror stories, no cost overruns (other than the ones that I requested), no delays, and no hassles. Everything was taken care of for me. That was priceless.

The End Result

Robert and Thomas, along with the builders, created what I consider to be the perfect home. Even though the house is finished, everyone involved in its creation is still available to answer questions. The whole team is on call to help me learn to use things like the dishwashers or the fireplace or the appliances. Of course, there will always be dreams of alterations—new ideas and new uses for rooms. Life in families is filled with those kinds of changes. But the fundamentals remain. I love my home, and I love the shapes, the colors, and the furnishings. I love the look and feel of it. My mother would have liked it too, I'm sure."

Wrapping It Up

To summarize, your clients will probably be between thirty-five and sixty years old, own their own home, have kids in college or who recently graduated, and have a desire to see their space or project move forward in a professional manner. They will understand the relationship between professional and client and respect your position as an expert in your field. They will be interested in how you run your business and whether or not the money they invest in you will be used to purchase the goods and services ordered. By working together, you will discover that they have a keen interest in different types of style and design components. You will bring all these disparate parts together in a way that will never be repeated in exactly the same manner. To see a project move forward to a satisfactory conclusion for you and your client is an exciting part of this business. Selecting the best possible clients for your business requires thought and integrity. You will continually assess what defines the optimum client and will find that definition may change from time to time. You will grow as a designer and your firm will prosper. By finding a well-managed client you will also discover the optimum interior designer within.

CHAPTER TWO
MARKETING TO THE CLIENT

"First it is necessary to stand on your own two feet. But the minute a man finds himself in that position, the next thing he should do is reach out his arms."
— Kristin Hunter, *O Magazine*, November 2003

Now that you have determined who your optimum clients are, comprehensive and effective marketing and public relations plans are essential to reaching those clients. Many interior design firms simply select the best photographs of recent installations, buy advertising in the local or regional shelter magazines, insert their address and telephone number, and call that a marketing plan. In today's competitive world of modern interior design marketing, that is nowhere close to what is needed. As a matter of fact, a photo in a magazine barely touches on the many facets of what is needed to successfully promote your business. The milieu of networking, public relations, and advertising for a business is far more complex than a four-color ad in a magazine. It's up to you to decide how, when, and where you will reach out to your current and prospective clients. You should also be mindful of the cost of each different segment of outreach and which are most effective. Most successful design firms use a combination of different marketing and advertising strategies. A complete understanding of both marketing and advertising will help you decide what is right for your business and when the application of each is appropriate.

Networking

In the interior design game, who you know is just as important in gaining exposure and growing your business as what you know and how skillful you are. A network of friends, colleagues, and mentors is one of the important tools for your success. You will also find your clients are a significant part of your networking advantage in the marketplace. Your clients will be a large part of the old "word of mouth" marketing you've heard so much about. A clear message is important in creating good "word of mouth" throughout your network. What your clients tell their friends and how they tell it will take you far in this particular aspect of marketing. As we will discuss later in this chapter, the other components of marketing will also have an impact on your message. Understanding the individual pieces of the overall concept of marketing and public relations is part of good client management and promotion.

As with all aspects of marketing, creating and implementing a networking strategy that will benefit you and your firm is very important. An excellent choice might be to partner with key referral sources. These sources might include realtors, architects, builders, and contractors who already do business with your target clientele. In this instance your marketing will be directed at them, and your message should contain benefits for *them* that show how you can help *them* be more successful in their businesses. In some instances, it might also be appropriate to offer an incentive for referrals to potential clients. A relationship with these key individuals based on excellent service and mutual benefit for the client will result in the easiest and best leads. These can be invaluable contacts, ensuring that clients call you ready to hear what you can offer because the referral partner has spoken so highly of you and your firm.

Your network will also include members of numerous trade, civic, and professional organizations. Although in many instances you will be talking to people in the same business as you, it is still important to convey as succinctly as possible the networking message you would like to be circulated. Within each of these types of organizations are members who will talk about you and what you offer as a professional. Their clients, friends, and family are an extended network to whom you want to speak. Members of the organizations you join will take your message to them. Their family and friends will then send your message out to their friends and colleagues. Remember, good news as well as bad travels through your network. It has been said that for every good message spoken along a network as many as six bad might be spoken. You never want your message to become simple gossip. Maintain a consistent stream of good news for people to share about you and your business. Let them know when you create a new division within your firm, when you hire a new employee, and what awards you might be receiving. All of these types of news are worthy of repeating and will enhance your standing in the community. Don't inundate your network with a constant stream of uninteresting items or gossip. Make sure what you share speaks to your acumen as a businessperson and professional, and don't try to fill the airwaves with a constant stream of chatter.

What a Tangled Web We Weave

Within the context of networking are social networking sites, such as LinkedIn, Facebook, Allvoices, Twitter, and more. Each of these has endless opportunities and each offers a slightly different focus. There are tie-ins between most of the sites and, if you wanted, they could be your twenty-four-hour news service. Be aware, however, these sites can also use up a lot of your valuable time. Each must be managed in a way that is beneficial to your business and not a drain on your billable hours. As with all the other aspects of your business, time management is critical to the successful implementation of these social networking sites. Don't get lost in the minutiae of who saw what, when, and where they may be going. As with word of mouth, your posts to the site should be about your success as a businessperson and professional, not simple chitchat.

I have found that LinkedIn seems to be more directed toward business and business owners. It allows you to tell the world about your business without a lot of personal information. Yes, they do ask about your education, where you grew up, and what type of organizations you belong to, but the focus still tends more toward business. This site also allows you to have your blog uploaded directly to your page, thereby sharing it with everyone to whom you are linked. This creates another opportunity for your blog to help with the dissemination of your message. LinkedIn, like most of the others, also allows you to link to your e-mail whenever any one person, group, or business posts to the site.

Allvoices is all about what is happening right now in our country and the world. Its major sub-topics include business, politics, science and technology, sports and much, much more. As with all the other sites mentioned, the "news" is posted by individuals interested in whatever particular subject you click on. You are also invited to contribute. Some of the business news is current and particularly helpful for entrepreneurs and those interested in the business of business.

Facebook may just be the granddaddy of them all. With millions of members all over the world you connect to people you didn't even know you knew. Between videos, photos, and links to other people and sites you could simply lose yourself in the pages of this monster social networking site. Created by two guys in college for their small group of friends, Facebook has expanded to include luminaries, actors, politicians, and those who simply want to be noticed. A very interesting recent development with this site is the enormous number of baby boomers and older participants who have decided to join. This group may be part of your optimum client base, so management of this site could become crucial to your overall marketing strategy. It can't and shouldn't be the only way for you to distribute your message, but it just might be one of the best. It's up to you to decide.

When properly managed, each of these sites offers ways to broadcast your message. They are a great way to inform anyone listening just what is happening in your particular business world. You will need to make sure the people you want to contact in this way know they have the opportunity to join all the sites. Many will find it fun and interesting to be part of this continual feed of information. Some may decide to drop the whole thing after a while but most will remain members and continue to get your feed when you post to whichever site you choose.

Don't Get Blogged Down

The last piece of this particular puzzle is your own blog. A blog, short for Web log, is essentially an online journal that you can update with regular posts about your business. Blog posts can be interesting for you to write and informative for your clients. They can also include photographs and color-specific articles and images. If you write about topics that clients find interesting, valuable, or simply fun to know, you will keep them coming back for more. As with all marketing the object is to position yourself as an expert in the field of interior design. You help define your firm and yourself as the "go-to" person when it comes to questions about interior design, industry news, and the latest trends. A blog can become more than a simple tool for communication between you and your client. Taken to the next level, a blog should educate, motivate, and, hopefully, inspire. Yes, inspire. You might also consider using your blog to talk to a larger audience than your prospective clients. A larger, more general audience will also help you position your business within a larger framework of business endeavors and entrepreneurialism. I created a blog in late 2007 to bring attention to my business and the book I was in the process of writing. As I discovered, blog posts need not be overlong nor do they have to touch on multiple topics within each given subject. The following example shows how quickly a blog can make its point without rambling on and on.

"Blog # 13: The Ladies Who Lunch

I am always amazed at how many 'ladies' spend every workday having lunch with their clients. Not only are they in the design center working with the client, but they also stop for an hour or more to have a bite. Is that a good way to use our very valuable time? Is it a good way to spend our clients' design time dollars? I think not. Interior design is a business, not an avocation. We, as professionals, should use the design center to source our projects, not as a testing ground for clients' reactions to certain furniture and fabrics. We should be secure in the knowledge that our decisions will meet the design criteria for the project, and we need not produce more than two, three, or four selections for any given element. As the 'ladies' spend hours in a social whirl with Mrs. GotRocks instead of producing the given project, it becomes evident to all concerned that the project will probably drag on forever. Decisions are delayed and selections not made. For the client, who generally doesn't know any better, frustrations may build to a point that confrontation is inevitable. For the 'lady' designer, profit slips through her fingers and she just can't understand why the bills aren't getting paid. I would advocate this 'lady with taste' move on to the bridge table and let some talented young designers show her how it's done. As a teacher of business practices for interior designers, I find more and more young designers getting the message about business. Yes, green design is all the rage but without a profitable business none of that 'green' is going to grow. So stop having lunch with every client that comes down the pike and produce the project in a timely and profitable manner. Repeat after me, interior design is a business."

I was actually discovered by the publisher of this book and our first book, *Starting Your Career as an Interior Designer* through the blog I was writing. So, although my goal was simply to talk to an audience about interior design, I created a blog and book component to my business that continues to support our aims of superior quality, luxury residential interior design.

Your blog will also keep people talking about you and your firm. For some of you, posting weekly will be the best option. Others of you may find that updating your blog twice a month or even monthly is all you can manage to maintain the quality you want. Whether you post daily, weekly, monthly, or simply from time to time be sure to let the right people know when and where to find your latest update. Need inspiration? Try talking about how to clean new upholstery, or where the best designer showrooms are and how to access them. Bring new products to the attention of your readers. Industry news can be exciting, and you might want to post updates about what colors the Color Council has decreed are in vogue. Write about whatever you think will attract attention and help position you as an expert in our very diverse field. Generally, the pieces you create shouldn't be too personal and shouldn't contain items unrelated to the interior design profession.

Newsletters Go the Way of Dinosaurs

Similar in content to a blog, a business newsletter is an old standby for many interior design firms. You may decide to have yours printed, but more and more interior designers are sending newsletters over the Internet. Not only do you show sensitivity to the environment, but you also have the chance to maintain a current e-mail address list for your clientele. The newsletter should contain the same ingredients as your word of mouth message and be interesting, easy to read, and not more than about four pages. As more and more designers move on to blogs for the immediate dissemination of information, the newsletter just may go the way of mauve and grey color combinations for interior design. Replacing your newsletter with your blog is easy and allows you to maintain a more cutting-edge appeal for most of your clients.

Positioning

All designers have to decide how, when, and where to present themselves to the public. This is called positioning. It is essential that as a designer you understand that the way you present yourself in public (for example, at an event or within a certain social or professional circle) will reflect on your brand (more about that later). Be careful and consistent with your positioning because you are not just presenting yourself as an individual, you are also presenting yourself as a professional brand. As you begin to reach out to prospective clients and communicate with current clients, the need for a clear and unmistakable position in the community is imperative. The image you create both in dress and manner will be part of your positioning plan. This clear and consistent image helps you control how clients will respond to you and your ideas.

It's Not an Act

The concept of positioning is closely aligned with your business persona. Your persona is the public role or character you assume as a professional interior designer. It is not a mask, nor is it a sham. Your professional persona is reflected in how you treat other people and how you expect to be treated. Your persona need not be snobby, aloof, or inaccessible. It's not a performance, and it is something you will need to be comfortable being. Notice I said being, not acting. Your persona is an enhanced version of you. For some, their persona will be their personality with the volume turned way up. For others, their persona will be very closely related to the person they have always been. It's up to you to define how you want to present yourself in the world of modern interior design. How you position your business and the persona you adopt for the business is how clients will relate to you and your business. Create an image you enjoy and are comfortable with.

Public Relations

Public relations is the second tier of marketing, involving an individual or business strategically exposing services to the public in order to create positive buzz, or word of mouth, in the marketplace. Public relations can be as simple as talking to friends at the supermarket or as complex as staging a two-day trunk show at a local hotel or club. This part of your marketing strategy can be a lot of fun and very serious business at the same time. In this particular arena it is up to you to create the "buzz" about your business. This leads directly to what every good interior design firm wants: good word of mouth.

Lend Me Your Ears

When you stage a seminar, trunk show, or other event open to the public, you are also setting the stage to present your best possible side to your audience. Public speaking is one of the best and most exciting ways to advertise your services. The people who attend your event will talk about it to their friends and those friends will talk about it to others. Kathryn Long of Ambiance Interiors in Asheville, North Carolina, relates her experiences when she was just starting out in the business.

"When I started my business in 1977, I researched specific clubs in the community with largely or exclusively female members. I chose to speak to several garden clubs around the area and decided to show fabrics and wall coverings that had not been previously available in Asheville, North Carolina. It would have been wonderful to present photographs of my work but there weren't any then; I had just opened my doors. I also explained the importance of ASID and the difference between a professional designer and a self-proclaimed decorator. Many of the women at my seminars had never worked with an interior designer and were very interested in my approach to educating the consumer as to the importance of working with a trained professional. I, of course, pointed out I was an active member of ASID and a professional interior designer. The seminars positioned me in the community as an expert in interior design and several of the women I met through these talks are still clients.

Networking never ends. It is difficult to imagine how a person who does not enjoy meeting people could succeed as a professional interior designer.

Belonging to nonprofit organizations such as the Symphony Guild or the local Preservation Society are important platforms for you as well as wonderful support for the community in which you live. Business organizations such as Rotary and your local Chamber of Commerce also help with networking. Join an organization that appeals to you and that you find interesting and exciting. No matter what group you join you should have a sincere interest in its activities and a desire to become involved with the people who are members. It means meeting people and having an opportunity to talk about my business.

My firm has, over the years, held many of our functions at our office and at the homes of very satisfied clients. As a matter of fact, an event in a client's home was probably the party that created the most direct success for me. An architect I now work with on a regular basis attended the party and began recommending me to his clients shortly after. He had been working with another designer who was living in the middle of the resort area where he does most of his work but she married a client and moved to Texas. I had also been sending this architect a Christmas card every year for the past several years and I'm sure that did not hurt.

At the moment, I am opening a new office in an historic home in Asheville that my firm is renovating. This is an exciting opportunity for me to showcase my firm's work and allow public access to this iconic property. It is also a wonderful chance to meet new friends and network with existing clients; and that is a good thing."

The marketing opportunities in any community are almost unlimited. Between clubs, residential communities, service organizations, and your own productions you could be speaking somewhere in your town almost once a week. It's relatively free advertising and you get to create and deliver the message yourself.

Overcoming Your Fears

I know many interior designers who find speaking before a large group intimidating. There are, of course, a number of ways to overcome what is essentially stage fright. Although you might feel as if you are dying when you step in front of a crowd, the chances are very slim you will actually expire. Most accomplished speakers were once frightened novices and learned techniques to help them get beyond their discomfort. With the right kind of speaking techniques your audience won't notice your sweaty armpits or shaky knees.

Toastmasters International is well-known in the public speaking arena and, to quote their Web site, "is a world leader in helping people become more competent and comfortable in front of an audience." The meetings of local chapters are usually no larger than twenty participants and are designed to encourage comfort and ease when speaking in public. Often you will meet other business leaders from around your area who want to improve their skills for presentations. Your peers critique your performance with a focus, primarily, on what you did correctly. Suggestions for improvement in specific areas help you become more comfortable with your stage presence and able to perform competently.

Most universities and colleges offer courses in public speaking or speech. More formal in approach and usually without a lot of peer review, these classes can also help you improve as a public speaker. These courses are not geared for business people, and you might find the average age of the students a little intimidating. Still, the skills taught and the amount of actual speaking will help you overcome many of your perceived shortcomings.

While you're on campus you might consider taking an acting class or two. Yes, acting. These courses encourage expression in ways not found in any of the other venues I've discussed, and you just might find in this setting the opportunity to let your outgoing personality soar. Beginning classes teach about posture, speech projection, movement, and concentration. As you progress you may be asked to roll around on the floor, mime a particular movement, or create a character far different from your own. As you begin to relax in front of the class and perform these outrageous tasks, you might find you are more comfortable with yourself, and that will translate into an ability to be at ease in front of any audience.

Whatever path you choose to increase your comfort zone will also help with client management and employee relations. You will have a more commanding presence in public and that, in turn, will translate to a more relaxed and comfortable presentation, whether speaking to a large audience or a single client.

Advertising

Effective advertising is the repetitive delivery of a consistent message related to a quality product. Advertising is also something for which you will need to pay. You select exactly what will be said, how it will be said, and to whom it will be said. The demographic structure of the viewers of a particular publication, radio, or television show will dictate whether or not it is the right venue for your message. With this type of advertising you are also talking to a lot of people who will not be interested or can't afford your services. The more focused the media you select the more tightly directed your message will be. You will also find with that cost will rise with a more focused approach.

Right on Target

Interior designers, generally, don't include direct marketing in their arsenal of marketing techniques, but it can be very effective in reaching the clients you need to succeed. Direct marketing is not just "junk mail." It requires a comprehensive plan and a well-conceived piece to interest prospective clients and bring your message to the people who would use your services.

I've asked Tanya Shively, ASID, of Sesshu Design Associates, Ltd., Scottsdale, Arizona, to again give us some insight, this time into direct marketing.

"Marketing directly to your ideal clients is easier than you might think. Taking out an ad in a magazine or other publication is often not your best avenue. Advertising in magazines tends to be too general, very expensive, and does not create a very high return on investment (ROI). You don't have a lot of control over who sees your ad. Sending out your message directly to those people you have identified as your best clients is far more easily accomplished through direct marketing.

The key to successfully marketing directly to anybody, whether it is a potential client or a key referral source, is your list. Your success is only as good as the list you mail to. Luckily, this is very easy to compile. There are many companies that can provide you with a mailing list that can be highly targeted to your specific ideal market. They can select names based on zip codes, income level, occupation, age, marital status, interests, length of residence in their home, and many more criteria. Costs vary for this so check several sources. Google is a great source for finding these companies. Many online printing services, such as Modern Postcard, also provide mailing lists as an optional add-on to printing services.

There are many ways to accomplish direct marketing, but large, oversized, colorful postcards seem to be the most cost effective and produce the best ROI. The advantage to a postcard is that while most people easily recognize and immediately throw out junk mail, they at least glance at postcards and the message is right there and visible. With a great message that speaks to their needs, you stand a better chance of getting a call or other action from them. Other options that make an impact are large, impressive packages, maybe priority mail or FedEx, and brochures that mail without an envelope. The drawback to these options is mainly cost, which reduces your ROI. With the typical interior design client's substantial lifetime value, this may not be a negative. It all depends on your plan and extent of your budget to execute your total marketing strategy. Keep in mind that it will often take between seven and nine contacts from you before a potential client will take action and call for an appointment, so you will need to multiply the cost of any single marketing piece by seven to determine your true cost. One mailer sent out is not very likely to generate a substantial or sufficient response.

When marketing directly to your ideal clients, you should use your USP (Unique Selling Proposition) to create a message that speaks to what they want from you. Any marketing message, no matter what form or where it's placed should always keep in mind the old rule of WIIFM—"What's In It For Me?"—from clients' perspectives. When they read your ad, they are asking themselves, either consciously or subconsciously, "What is in this for me? Why should I call them? How does this fix my problem?" Be sure that whether you hire a copywriter or do it yourself, your message speaks directly to them, addresses their needs, and illustrates how your services benefit them and attend to their needs. One good method for this is to imagine you are talking with them in person, one on one. Answer their questions as simply as possible, without using jargon or designer speak."

Direct marketing can be a valuable asset to your overall campaign to let the world know who you are and what you do. When done with style and panache, direct marketing can bring you clients who might otherwise not even know you exist.

The Printed Page

Most professional interior design firms have been using print advertising to reach out to clients for a number of years. Where you advertise and with whom are important decisions and, as you will find, costly. The beautiful color photographs you choose to include in your print advertising should be among your very best and most recent work. For many design firms, full page, four-color images are the optimum choice for magazine advertising. Other firms have found smaller ads are sufficient. Whatever you choose, your ad should show the full range of styles you have to offer. Advertising must be a consistent message sent out regularly to be successful—once a year won't cut it. The larger the magazine and the broader the reach, or distribution, the more expensive the placement cost. Planning your campaign is important, and you want to make sure your brand is evident in each ad.

The look should be consistent with your overall image. The ad should be recognizable and memorable as coming from your design firm.

Advertising in daily and weekly newspapers might also be a way to reach your optimum client. It's not as sexy and exciting as color print advertising, but this black and white approach is far more inexpensive and gives you the ability to repeat your message more often for the same amount of money. I wouldn't suggest you try to use images in black and white as they will simply look fuzzy and unclear. This type of advertising is more effective when you use text to tell your story. It can be more along the lines of what is called an "advertorial" in the trade and might have the look of an editorial or news piece. The difference is you create the message about your company rather than some unknown reporter.

Branding

Now that I've got you plotting innovative advertising campaigns, let's spend some time with advertising's smoother older brother, branding, as this is the spirit behind the marketing operation. No, we aren't talking about branding cattle; we're referring to the process of developing an image for your business that can be conveyed through your marketing initiatives. Technically speaking, branding is the promotion of a particular product or company by means of advertising and distinctive design. The essence of branding is a total understanding of you and your firm and what you want the world to see and believe about your organization.

Brand is distinctly different from position. Your brand is related to your image and how your firm looks to the world. You will have positioned your business in a particular niche of the market and the brand is what people will remember when thinking of your firm.

Be the Brand

Your brand is reflected in everything from your stationery to what you wear and with whom you're seen. It is the style of your business and requires a commitment to "being the brand" every day of your professional career. You, your employees, and the firm need to present a consistent and uniform face to the world for brand success. Branding is building an image and sticking to it as you expand and acquire new clients. You need to believe in your brand and project a genuine energy every time you step out. Your brand should be focused on what you believe your optimum client will be looking for in an interior designer. Will you have a clean, crisp, tailored look? Will you be a little more outgoing and dress in today's most stylish clothing? If you believe large hats, outré shoes, and outlandish scarves will attract your optimum client, then by all means dress that way. Most upscale clients, however, are looking for something just a little more conservative. A brand that is easy to maintain, in which you believe, will be one of the most effective sources of referral and business for your firm.

Don't Fear Evolution

Once you've decided on a brand, never stop working on improving it. Many brands, retail stores, automobiles, magazines, and others have morphed into something uniquely different from what they were when they began. If you think of the personality Cher as a brand, review how her brand image has changed over the years. She moved from a sixties singer, to television performer, to Academy Award-winning actress, to pop icon. Hers was and is a wonderfully exciting and diverse career and is a perfect example of the way brands can be changed and refined to reflect the demands of the public.

Your business, too, will be able to adapt and change with each passing year. You will define what is needed to succeed in any particular arena and time. What works at this moment may not work three years from now. Be prepared to continually assess the needs of your company and stay up-to-date on what your clientele wants.

From This Moment On

Each journey begins with the first step, and using the tools I've given you, that step should be easier for you and your firm to take. With four major divisions within the marketing arena, start with a plan that utilizes each division to its best advantage and to the success of your firm. Each segment of marketing is a variation on how to best present your business to the community and win the respect and loyalty of current and prospective clients. Your innate ability to understand what is best for your firm's image will enable you to create a diverse, interesting, and productive marketing campaign. This has always been a favorite part of my job, and I hope you will find the real joy that comes from producing an effective and beautiful marketing campaign.

CHAPTER THREE
THE INITIAL INTERVIEW

"The meeting of two personalities is like the contact of two chemical substances: If there is any reaction, both are transformed."
— Carl Jung (1875 – 1961)

The exhilaration of creating and implementing an exciting marketing plan will surely be followed by telephone calls from those prospective clients to whom you reached out. Now is the time to think about what you will say once you have them on your crafty marketing hook. The best place to start is to write down a few lines about your firm's attributes, successes, and awards. You might want to highlight the educational background of your staff or you may include a short list of high-profile clients. Include a list of your most recently completed projects, including geographic locations. By disclosing the location you will, quite often, give the prospect a sense of the scope of the project and level of finish. Once you've completed the list, reduce it a bit and think about possibly including one of the tidbits in your voicemail message. Keep your notes close to the telephone for a quick reference when you are speaking to a prospect.

First Impressions
Once the marketing kicks in and the telephone rings, be ready. The telephone call is your first step toward successful client management. As with all first impressions, this is your chance to make a unique statement about you and your business. Create a short greeting, add the title of

your new book or a tidbit of information about recent awards or participation in a community event, and have your receptionist practice a few times before speaking to a client. The greeting should be succinct and interesting; keep it around thirty seconds. The same rules apply whether the telephone is answered in person or by an answering machine. If you have decided to create the message for your company's answering machine, decide whether your voice is good for the tape, if you should hire a professional, or possibly look for someone within your office who might have just the voice image for your firm. When preparing to record the message, turn off all music or other audio instruments that might be picked up by the microphone. The person doing the recording should also be sure to smile as they read the script. I'm not kidding about smiling while creating a message. Try it a few times with and without the smile and you'll agree.

Your telephone interviewing technique should include asking for callers' names if they don't introduce themselves. I have found over the years that a client who introduces himself immediately tends to be the easiest with which to work. Ask how you can help, then let him explain what he has in mind. Don't jump in immediately with answers to questions that haven't been asked. Though you will already know what questions you would like to ask, let the client feel he has the lead.

Once the client has slowed down, you will be able to ask the questions necessary to feel comfortable proceeding. You should ask how the client heard about your firm. It's always important to ascertain what type of marketing, promotion, or advertising is working best for your firm. Be sure to jot down the answer to this very important question. It will help you define where you might want to increase exposure or reduce your commitment to a particular newspaper or magazine. It will also help you know whether or not your word of mouth marketing is working. Try to find out if the client has used an architect or interior designer before, and if so, ask about the quality and success of that collaboration.

As you lead the conversation to the project, define again its scope. Try to find out whether or not construction is involved and, if so, how far along the process is. If the client hasn't already contacted a builder, you might suggest your services include a contractor who works on your team. If he is asking you to jump into the middle of a project and will need instant design choices, be wary of whether or not you will be able to get and maintain control of the client. He is coming to you already out of control and might be expecting miracles. Budget, of course, will be important, and if the client isn't forthcoming, you might simply ask for a range. Ask about the project timeline and whether or not a non-negotiable date of completion has been set. Should you decide to set a meeting for the initial interview, ask if the client has photos or samples from magazine articles to help give you a sense of what he has in mind for the project. Ask if you will be meeting at the project site or somewhere else. With new construction and major renovations, it is not always feasible to meet on location for the first time. You will, of course, want to see the project before you sign any contracts.

Don't Forget to Follow-Up

Before ending the conversation make sure you have first and last names of all involved, the address of the project, and, if different, the address where you will meet. Set a time for the meeting and explain you will be sending out a small packet with information about your firm. Yes, you should follow-up with a mailing of some sort to prepare the prospective client for the initial meeting. It can be a CD with photos of other jobs you have completed or a three-fold brochure. Another note about the timing of the meeting: don't rush out that afternoon or the next day. It isn't a good idea to have the prospect think you aren't busy. Give it at least forty-eight hours. This will give you enough time to Google the prospects' names and find out a little about who you are going to meet. Don't roll your eyes at me. It's not unethical; it's good business practice. Also be sure to let someone in your office know where the appointment is or leave a note on your office calendar.

It's important here to make another point about the meeting. Don't ever go out on an appointment on Sunday. You, like everyone else, are entitled to a day off. I often take appointments for Saturday morning but rarely for Saturday afternoon. Even couples who want to interview also want some time on their own, and Saturday afternoon appointments invariably have the clients running late or canceling at the last minute. It's your choice, of course, what days and how you would like to work. Just don't change those days to accommodate prospects who can't meet any time except on Sunday or other times you have declared as off time. If you do, you will lose control of the client and the project.

To Fee or Not to Fee

You will have already decided whether or not you will charge for the first appointment. It's your business and it's up to you. I know many designers who will not leave the office for any reason without charging. I, on the other hand, never charge for the initial interview. I believe a meeting with no obligation on either side helps everyone be a little more relaxed. I also have no problem, should the prospect be in some way unacceptable as a client, walking away from the meeting without sending out a letter of agreement or a contract. This interview is as much for you as it is for the prospect. Never feel you have to take the job just because you went on the interview. There will always be other prospects but once you've saddled yourself with a couple who might not be the best fit for you and your firm it becomes very difficult to manage them or the project.

Client control and management is first and foremost about self-discipline. Don't waver in your focused goal of being the very best designer and business person you can be. With that in mind you will position yourself ahead of the pack when it comes to your ability to manage projects and clients. As a professional you will have prepared an agenda of what you want to accomplish at the initial interview. In the beginning you might write down the agenda but after a few dozen interviews you will have a good idea of what needs to be covered.

Prepared and on Time

Though it may be a cliché your mother always told you, it's true that you never get a second chance at a first impression. In our business it can make or break a new relationship. Seriously consider the impression you want to make on these new prospective clients. At the appointed time be prompt, well-groomed, and prepared. If you're early, wait outside in the car for a few minutes, but don't be late. Dress fashionably without being outlandish. Ultra-short skirts, tight pants, or hair that is dyed purple and punked-out usually doesn't work for the kind of professional client with whom you will want to work.

First impressions are so very important to client management that you should have a standard style of dress you know looks good on you and is stylish without being outré. Depending on the area of the country in which you live, a jacket and tie, or even a suit, might be the best choice for a first meeting. Your clothing should be stylish, fashionable, and properly fitted. Take the time needed to select the proper clothing and, if you've gained a few pounds, adjust the selections accordingly. Keep in mind that when dealing with high-end clients cheap clothing doesn't work. Shoes should be polished and the style should be appropriate for the occasion. Now that you are the fashionable professional you know you can be, get ready to meet the potential client.

Greet prospects with a firm, but not too tight, handshake and let them lead you into the space. Place your briefcase on the floor next to your chair, never on a table or piece of furniture. You might scratch it and that just wouldn't do. If you think all this fuss before you even start the interview isn't important, you are sadly mistaken. All of this helps you set the tone

41

for the upcoming meeting, define you as the professional in charge, and illustrate your ability to manage not only the project but also the client.

Preliminary Questions

Once you're seated it's time for you to fire away with the questions you will need to ask before you decide to accept the project. Which space or area is to be renovated? How is the space used and will that use change after the project is completed? How many people are in the family? You can then move on to general likes and dislikes in the way of color, fabric, finish, and style. Don't get too specific about design solutions. You're not trying to be secretive, you simply want to make sure any solution you propose is appropriate for the family, space, and project. As intellectual property, your ideas are valuable and shouldn't be thrown around willy-nilly. Client control begins with this interview, and your questions and answers will lay the foundation for all that is to come. Be concise and don't try to "hard sell" prospects about your firm and its attributes. You do, however, want to make sure they understand the scope of your expertise and to prove you are the best fit for the proposed work. Don't try to overwhelm prospects with your design knowledge. Use words and phrases they will understand. Never talk down to prospects.

Take a hard look at the space in which the interview is conducted. Is it tidy and well kept? If not, you should know you might have problems later in the project. Prospective clients who maintain an organized and well kept home are clients who generally will want a project to move forward in a timely and efficient manner. Rooms that are in disarray and have an unkempt look reflect the cluttered mindset of the occupants and give you a clear indication of just how much control will be needed to keep a project on track and on budget.

Also pay attention to how focused the prospects are on the interview. If they constantly interrupt the proceedings to answer cell phones, don't turn off the television when you arrive, or haven't seen to it the children are cared for while you are there, you might be in trouble. These interruptions are a clear indication that they do not value you as a professional and will not easily respect your judgment as the project progresses. Interior design is not brain surgery, but it does require everyone to work together to create the new interiors.

Marlene Oliphant, ASID, of Marlene Oliphant Designs, LLC, in Glendale, California, works in residential interior design and shares her perspective on first interviews.

"The first half-hour is free of charge. This is my chance to take a look at the room or larger project, explain how I work, and let them know what my charges will be. I ask them what they would like to achieve with the meeting, guide them through an overview of the project, and take a look, if possible, at the space to be designed. I dissuade them from an in-depth description of everything they might want for the project; that is left for the actual consultation. During this short thirty-minute conversation I discuss how we might work together and I give them a few tips and ideas on how the project might proceed. I never give away exactly how the project would be designed. If they ask how I might arrange the furniture or what kind of kitchen layout I would provide, I explain those questions are best answered after measurements have been taken and I have the layout on paper. I let them know I need a chance to review the entire project before arriving at the best possible solution. Good client management does not include design solutions given off the cuff, and this process also ensures any intellectual property you share comes only after the letter of agreement or contract has been signed.

Are They Worthy?

After the first half hour, I ask prospective clients if they feel they received value from the discussion. If they are interested in continuing I tell them we are beginning the paid portion of the consultation. I have previously discussed fees and explained that the first thirty minutes was at no charge. I have also let them know that my initial retainer or consultation fee is $300.00 for a minimum of two hours with any additional hours billed at $150.00 per hour. If they choose to proceed at that moment, I take a check for the time spent on that day, then send out a letter of agreement for the project along with a questionnaire for the client to complete and return.

There are also other questions I ask during the initial interview to ascertain the potential of the prospective clients. I ask if they watch HGTV and, if so, which programs. I explain to them the budgets and timelines are not realistic—the programs are, after all, entertainment. If there are differences in taste between the couple I ask how those differences were handled in the past. We again discuss the budget and I suggest a ten percent cushion for those items they will simply have to have during the course of the project. I ask to see the rest of the house and note the colors, style, finishes, and furnishings throughout. I also take note of the style and type of clothing the prospective clients are wearing during the interview. Any twinges, things that bother you or red flags that pop up, even if you can't put a finger on why, should all be duly noted in this interview. Like a first date, people are usually on their best behavior. The real characteristics generally come out when you spend some time asking questions and letting them talk. A lot of schmoozing is necessary to draw people out to try to get to know them a little better.

Sorry, I'm All Booked

If, during the interview, I decide I don't want this project, I tell them my current schedule won't allow a new project at this time. Or, I tell them the particular style they want is not my forte and will recommend someone else I feel might be better suited to their project. If their budget is very low or the quality they are interested in is not up to my firm's standards, I recommend they use me for a simple consultation and pursue the rest of the project on their own or through a retail or cabinet store.

My own experience has taught me how important the interview with prospective clients is. I once interviewed an older woman, a widow, who wanted her home office redone. I did the initial interview, gave her a letter of agreement, and she paid my retainer. I began going through my usual questionnaire with her to determine what she wanted. She had shown me a Staples catalog for the office furniture, but I told her that I would not be utilizing their furnishings and would, instead, use a higher quality of furnishings for her office. Her taste and budget mandated the change. After I had been questioning her for about five minutes about her style, she stopped and said, 'I don't know why you are asking me all these questions; I've already told you what I want.' I should have stopped right there and handed back her check. But, I was a new designer, working for myself, and I wanted the business. I told her I was just trying to get to know her and her style, as we were complete strangers before that day. Well, she turned out to be quite a cranky person through the whole project. She was very impatient and didn't understand why I couldn't set up her DSL along with the desk. It was a very unpleasant experience, I had to wait eight weeks for the furniture to arrive and get the balance due from that installation and resign from the job. This experience taught me that my intuition is very accurate. I just knew going in that I should not have taken on this job from the very beginning!"

No Compatibility

Designers across the country use different techniques to ascertain which clients might become problematic during the course of a project. Prospective clients give you all sorts of indications about whether or not they will be fun to work with, good clients, and able to make decisions in a timely manner. During your initial interview it's up to you to determine whether or not you want to work with them. During the course of the conversation at the initial interview, if clients ask me more than three times about the budget and how expensive the project might be, I begin to think twice about whether or not they will actually be able to perform when we get right down to the nitty-gritty of contracts and letters of agreement. Some prospects simply can't come to terms with what items and design services cost in today's market and it's up to you to educate them or walk away. Other clients simply don't have the resources to bring the envisioned project to fruition. Again, it's up to you to either help them understand a larger budget is needed or refer them to another interior designer.

As mentioned earlier, the appearance of the home is important to your ability to make a decision as to whether or not a prospect will make an optimum client. Messy kitchens, bathrooms, and bedrooms indicate an unorganized and chaotic family life. That lack of organization will almost certainly roll over into the design process.

I once interviewed with clients, Mr. and Mrs. McGee, who had the budget in place and were ready to proceed. Molly explained over the telephone their desire to create a new kitchen and generally update the whole house. We discussed bathroom renovations and how walls might be moved to open up the space for a more workable area for living and dining. I was ready to move forward with them and set up an appointment to see the house.

The problem, for me, was the condition of the home. The original house contained three bedrooms, a bath, and a kitchen. In the late 1980s an addition was placed at the rear of the home with access through the kitchen. Not an ideal choice, and it was further compromised by a staircase leading to the second floor that was only thirty-two inches wide. The whole addition, including a three-car garage below, was finished in a style that would best be described as tract-home cheap and contained two bedrooms and two baths. The exterior was a jumble of overgrown plants and grasses with a driveway in desperate need of repaving. In two different areas walls had been removed and the floors had been left unfinished and untidy. The house, in general, was cluttered and in a state of disarray. In every room no space was left to move around the multitude of items and possessions. One room had books stacked floor to ceiling, two desks, three file cabinets, books stacked on three different tables, a music stand, saxophone, piano, and microwave oven. When I told them we wouldn't be able to create the library they wanted in this space without clearing it completely, they were aghast. Where, they asked, would they put all the items in the room while the work was being completed? Where, I asked, would they store all the items in all the other rooms while the proposed renovation was being done? They said they fully expected to be able to live in the home while the work was being done. When I explained I wouldn't suggest that as an option they continued to ask for other solutions. In short, they hadn't taken the time to consider the ramifications of the project they proposed to initiate. I decided not to take the job and was loathe to refer them to another design colleague.

A Team Approach

Since November 2003, Suzanna Lawler-Isco and her young and talented group have created interiors based on traditional interior design training with a cutting-edge, out-of-the-box mentality that fosters a pleasant and worry-free design process for her team and her clients. Lawler-Isco Interior Design, located in Winter Park, Florida, and Suzanna approach initial interviews as part of an overall process of client and project management.

"To create an initial interview technique for our offices we talked to Lloyd Princeton, principal consultant for Design Management Consultation, and referred to the book by Christine M. Piotrowski entitled *Professional Practice for Interior Designers.*

While there are many aspects to meeting a client and introducing oneself, an interview can be summed up to one word: expectations. By setting appropriate expectations that address each relationship throughout the process, you are much more likely to create an environment for success. All the key team members need to be addressed on some level to ensure your client fully understands the roles each will play as it relates to you, the designer. This includes the client, builder, architect, subcontractors, and the team members on your staff who will personally be attending to the project.

As to which relationship should be addressed first, I typically take my cue from the client. If he is consumed with thoughts of his home and wants to tell me his needs first, I let him. The client won't want to listen to me if he feels I haven't heard him. In the beginning, if the client asks questions about me and my firm, I show him my portfolio while I explain how my firm met former clients' expectations. This usually gets the client talking about his project as he sees things he likes or hears topics that peak his interest.

We Left the Pony at Home
One of the harder lessons for me to learn when I started interviewing clients was to have more of a flexible, give and take approach to the conversation instead of a well-rehearsed "dog and pony show." I was so consumed with trying to sell my talents and prove my knowledge that I'm sure I lost their attention at times. With the help of my partner, who has a degree in communications, I learned to edit

my discussions by taking time to hear what the client is saying and respond. For example, if a client starts talking about process and how a project will be coordinated, I pull out an example of a client notebook and show her how we organize all the information and what methods we use to communicate with architects, builders, and subcontractors. This sets the expectation that we are a firm that can efficiently project manage and will have the full vision of the finished spaces in mind throughout the process.

If a client is more concerned with the actual furnishings and design style, I spend my time going through the portfolio of previous work discussing manufacturers and what elements reflected former clients' tastes and how we were able to bring those elements to fruition. I discuss different styles and the process involved in determining which style might be used in a particular interior. I also discuss options for selecting furnishings, which might include design centers, markets, and antique vendors.

Although every now and again heaven drops a client in front of you who does not any have budget concerns, most do. While it isn't always the best idea to disclose your pricing during an initial interview, you can certainly discuss general ways you work with clients such as hourly versus a flat fee. I typically compare interior design to clothing from Ann Taylor, Gucci, and Versace or various cars by Toyota, Mercedes-Benz, and Bentley to imply different levels of quality, design, and cost. This gives a premise to discuss what the client's expectations are without discussing hard numbers.

Timelines are also a very important expectation that need to be addressed. There's an old saying, "Speed, quality, and budget—pick two." If a client wants a project fast-tracked, this certainly should be a factor when you are determining your pricing structure.

As I mentioned before, my partner goes with me to most interviews. While I focus on the conversation she focuses on body language, overall emotions, subtle hints to personality traits, and potential red flags that I often miss. Her input after the interview is invaluable. I highly recommend you have a team member go with you to help in such a way so that when you are determining pricing for a project, you have as much information as possible.

There are many lists available to you that suggest questions to ask, points to make, and lists of what to bring. We have developed a prospective client check list to help us remember all the important steps that we've gathered over the years. I suggest you make one of your own that will help you be more consistent and ensure you cover all the necessary topics. The topics on our list are:

1. Initial phone call
2. Research
3. Interview
4. Programming
5. Interview follow-up
6. Homework for the client

A couple of unusual points we include that you may not find on existing lists are asking the client how well he can visualize design concepts and what level of presentation he requires. Should the client require color boards or renderings, he should be made aware of the extra expense—however minimal compared to the overall investment he is about to make. Also ask what other specialists the client is considering hiring, such as a lighting designer.

Design on the Spot?

One last point I want to suggest is related to designing during the interview. Now that we have our design firm established, I do not offer much, if any, design advice during the interview. There are, however, a few exceptions to this rule. When we were first starting our business we had no portfolio to speak of, because we didn't own the rights to our designs done at other firms. The best way I could show my competency was to bring a scale and a roll of trash paper and ask to see their plans. By pointing out a handful of floor plan issues, I would prove my ability and have a platform to discuss all sorts of design aspects. This also worked well by inadvertently making the client feel we had already started working together. After that it seemed natural to sign a contract and continue the process. The only other situation in which I will now design in an interview is if an architect has brought me into a project and asked me to sit in on a meeting with the client. This is a great opportunity to show the client how your knowledge supplements the architect's strengths and how necessary the team approach is. I find this very effective.

Other quick notes to help you formulate your checklist: During the phone call, do a short interview. Set the date, time, and, most importantly, the length of the meeting. Most interviews should be conducted in an hour. Ask what other team members have already been selected, such as the architect and builder, so you can research them before the interview. Ask the client to bring any plans, pictures, and other collections to the interview to give you a general idea of what she is thinking for the project.

Should she ask you for a consultation in which you give design advice and are paid instead of an interview, be sure to quote her your rates and set a time and expectation limit.

Ask questions that concern the proposed project. You might ask how the client heard about you and your firm, why she feels the need for a designer, and what concerns she might have about the project in general. Remember, you are interviewing the client, too, and are looking for any clues that would help you decide whether or not this particular project will be a good fit for your firm.

Ask questions about the client's current home and the envisioned living space. Try to ascertain what design elements are most important, what rooms are most important, and how the new home differs from the existing residence.

Before leaving an interview, and based on the discussions during the interview, discuss what information you will be providing. You will define whether or not you will provide price quotes along with a contract and the time frame for making decisions and getting back in touch with one another.

Always send a thank you note to the potential client and whoever may have referred you. We usually send gourmet cookies to our faithful followers who are kind enough to suggest us to others."

Moving Forward

Assuming all goes well and you are happy with the prospects, at some point, usually after about forty-five minutes, the client will ask how to proceed—a phrase something like, "So, what's next? or "Where do we go from here?" That's your cue to discuss how your firm operates, what type of design retainer you will charge, and whether or not it will be billed back for the time required to create the presentation. Once you have explained the costs involved, invite the client to your studio for the second meeting. You will explain at that time that you expect him to sign the letter of agreement or contract you will send out, define precisely the scope of the proposed project, and discuss your retainer. Control of the project involves your ability to ask for and accept retainers and payments without being shy. Once you and your client are comfortable talking about money you will be that much closer to managing in a professional and efficient way.

Take your leave and return to your studio to review and transfer your notes to the newly created client file. If at all possible, don't wait until the next day. Create the notes while the interview is fresh in your mind. If, for any reason, you believe you have forgotten some part of the conversation or are unsure about exactly what was said, call the client immediately. Explain your need for clarification and ask about the aspect of which you are uncertain. Most prospective clients will respond to your inquiry easily and will respect you for ensuring every detail of the proposed project is clear in everyone's mind. You are now ready to prepare the letter of agreement or contract and set up the new client in your management software. Enjoy the end of a good day's work.

CHAPTER FOUR

SIGNING THE CONTRACT OR LETTER OF AGREEMENT

"A verbal contract isn't worth the paper it's written on."

— Samuel Goldwyn (1882 – 1974)

Now that you are ready to have the prospect sign on the dotted line, a look at your letter of agreement or contract is in order. As simple as it sounds there are designers out there who don't work with their clients in a professional manner or with signed contracts. That's not the best way to proceed. These instruments are an important aspect of client management and set the stage for the project to come. This document is the essence of how the project will proceed, and it should help you and your client align your expectations. It is through this document that you will explain your services, fees, procedures, and monetary expectations. Aligned expectations will make the project flow from the very beginning, and the contract is a wonderful way to describe how each of you will be most comfortable working together. Along with the letter of agreement or contract you might create a small one-page sheet of what the client should expect as the project moves forward. We have outlined on our Web site how the procedure works so it's easily accessible for our clients. The steps are defined and explained so the client will be well versed in what to expect as we move forward. This page need not be signed by the client but is for information purposes only.

Contracts vs. Letters of Agreement

Both a letter of agreement and a contract are binding legal documents and will become part of the client file. You will prepare these documents for review by your attorney. Once you are happy with the form, content, and intent of the document, review it one more time to be certain it is an equitable document. This will ensure that you are compensated for your work and the client receives what he believes he is due in the form of design services, furnishings, and fittings. Once you are satisfied, make the document part of your business process. This will also become what is known in the trade as a "boiler plate"—a document contained in your computer that will serve as a template to be used with each client. The term "boiler plate" refers to the fact that a majority of the content is not changed from client to client and is, therefore, like a steel plate—fixed and unchanging. These are the terms under which you will perform your contractual duties as an interior designer and client/project manager. Your ability to precisely outline what your firm will, and will not, do within the context of a project is important to good contracts and letters of agreement.

Contract or Letter: Which Is Better?

The real question is whether you want the in-depth coverage a contract provides or whether you prefer a more relaxed "gentleman's" type of agreement. Most interior design contracts actually begin with a letter of agreement or letter of understanding. It outlines the scope of the project without specific details about performance. Further details are attached to the document as contracts and addenda. No matter what you decide about letters of agreement versus contracts, be aware that both are an extension of your project management ability and a reflection of your company's business acumen. Your contract or letter also speaks volumes about your ethics and how you operate your business. Both instruments should be clear, concise, and up to date in terms of your firm's ability to perform its contractual duties.

Your Responsibilities

As the interior design project manager you are responsible for setting the parameters of your letter of agreement or contract. One of the first questions you will ask is, "Is a letter of agreement really a binding legal document?" Yes, it is. It is not, however, as comprehensive as a contract, and you should be aware of the many differences and shortcomings. I believe in the effectiveness of letters of agreement and have used them for years. One of the nice things about letters of agreement is their brevity. Most are no more than two pages and some as short as one. The example below defines the place and scope of the project, what will be required from the client both in terms of retainer and purchases, and how to move the project forward by signing the letter. When using a letter of agreement, there are often separate proposals for purchases, separate agreements between you, the client, and the contractor for contract work, and additional time charges for services outside the scope of the project as defined by the letter of agreement.

A Letter of Agreement

"We are pleased to submit this agreement for design consultation for your kitchen and other areas of your home on Morse Drive. Any third-party services by, among others, architects and engineers should be engaged directly by the client. Peninsula Interior Design will work in coordination with any third-party hired by the client. Peninsula Interior Design will be allowed to photograph both before and after images of the project to be used for promotion. The client's privacy will be ensured and the images will remain the property of Peninsula Interior Design.

We would appreciate a nonrefundable design fee of $5,000 on your account. You will be charged $250.00 per hour for design work, including consultations, space planning, shopping, planning the project, production, and delivery. Travel time out of the area will be charged at a fifty percent (50%) rate. The fees will be billed up to the amount of the retainer. Should additional time be required, additional fees will be charged as agreed upon by the designer and client. You will be entitled to twenty (20) hours of design time with the initial retainer. FedEx/UPS charges, if any, will be billed separately.

A written proposal will be prepared and presented to you for any purchases made through this office. Upon receipt of your written approval and a sixty percent (60%) deposit, your order will be placed. The balance of forty percent (40%) is due before receipt or installation of goods.

As acceptance of this agreement please sign and return a copy of this letter along with a check for the retainer to our office.

We appreciate the opportunity to work with you on this exciting project.

Robert Kingham_____
President, Peninsula Interior Design
Mr. and Mrs. John Friendly _____ Date_____ "

There are times, however, when I find a contract is a better choice for certain clients. Contracts are far more detailed, and it is up to you to make sure your contract is a perfect fit for your firm and the client. You need to describe clearly and exactly what is expected of your firm as well as what is expected of the client. Each of you must agree on the terms. A signature by both on the contract is sufficient and binding. Should your client arrive with his own contract, do not sign it. Have your attorney look over the document then amend your contract to reflect any changes you find acceptable from the client's contract. Once again, this is your business, and only in very rare instances do clients need to present a contract. If they insist you use their contract, you might want to let them walk.

There are many books available with pre-written contracts specifically for interior designers. One of the best is *Business and Legal Forms for Interior Designers,* from Allworth Press. The American Association of Interior Designers (ASID) also supplies to their members a comprehensive contract and letter of agreement. Whatever type of document you choose, be sure you review all aspects of what is promised and how it fits with your business. Even these examples are not carved in stone. They are meant to direct you and help you define your particular business needs to succeed financially and artistically.

Know the Project Details

The review of the contract or letter of agreement is essential to good client and project management. Your client is going to ask questions about the document and you need to know exactly what is included and what it means to the project. As contracts become more complicated there are so many aspects you will be asked about. You will include the scope of the project and how extensive your design concept services will be. At this point you will require a reta   iner of some sort, which will be applied to any time charges for concept services. Moving through the contract you will define what interior items will be supplied and whether or not your firm will purchase any or all items. If the client decides to purchase an item you specify from another firm, you may decide to require her to pay a percentage of the price paid as compensation for the time you spent working on that particular piece of furniture or installation. You might also consider a separate "item purchase agreement" to clearly define that particular aspect of the overall project.

Carol Parra-Little of Corporate Design Group, Inc., in Roseville, California, has created contracts that are concise and explain exactly how each party will be responsible for the efficient completion of the project. Carol also has supplied her perspective on how important the contract is and how it needs to be updated from time to time.

"I've enclosed a copy of our commercial contract and interior design services contract for Corporate Design Group, Inc. I don't know that they are terribly unique, but I feel our main points of clarification are as follows:

1. Consult an attorney to write the terms within the laws of the state in which you are working.

2. Be sure there is clarity as to:
   a. when fees are due
   b. what rate of interest will be charged if payment is not received on time
   c. storage fees if the project delivery date is delayed by the client
   d. who owns the goods if payment is not received
   e. who is responsible for attorneys fees in the case of a dispute
   f. issues pertaining to warranties
   g. how much clients will pay if they cancel the project and that the cancelation must be approved by seller (us).

A Commercial Design Contract

Our design proposals are written to cover some of the same issues as our contracts, but also include points that are quite different. Whenever possible, we try to outline both what is and what is not included in our services because it is important for a client to understand the entire process and exactly what the designer is providing. While it is virtually impossible to be sure the client fully understands what we (the designer) will be doing, we do our level best to educate and clarify the work we will be performing before the project begins. Spending time with the client at the beginning of the project to clarify all details of the project is time well spent.

The main points that I feel are important in the design contract are:

- clarifying the process and what the design team is providing
- noting the points at which client approval will be needed to proceed to the next step in the process
- clarifying fees for out-of-scope work requests
- noting our right to stop work if the client is not current with payments to the designer
- explaining how a client may go about terminating the contract
- identifying "additional services available"

We use the final section to outline services that may be needed in the project that are not included in the fixed fee scope (sometimes because the services were not requested in the clients' request for proposal, and including them would cause a competitive disadvantage). Another possible item in that section is "detailed furniture specifications." While we have provided for selections in our fixed fee package, if a client wants from us a list of detailed furniture specifications to use for the purpose of bidding, we charge an additional fee for that service because it takes more time to write a detailed shopping list than a furniture contract and purchase order.

If I were to summarize, I'd say that the contract (for either design or product) is vital to the life of the business. No work is done at my firm without a signed contract, because it leaves little to no ambiguity regarding what work or products we have committed to and for what price. Having clarity in our contracts tells the client how we do business, and we are consistent with that practice among all our clients. Since our terms are consistent and fair, if our terms do not suit a particular client, we are probably working with the wrong client. As a matter of fact, if we are already experiencing a resistance from the client at this stage of the process, the relationship is likely to be difficult, if not impossible, to manage going forward.

Corporate Design Group Master Design Proposal
April 1, 2009
Client's Name Here
#1 Client's Address Goes Here
Rancho Cordova, CA 95670
Attn.: Contact Name
Contract # D50330
Project: (address)

Interior Design Services

We are pleased to submit this proposal to provide interior design and project coordination services for your project located at (address). It is our understanding the overall project encompasses approximately (20,000 useable) square feet. For purposes of this proposal, our fees are specific to the interior finishes, furniture layout, and furniture relocation coordination only.

1. Design Development

1.1. Interview key personnel to develop requirements for the finishes and furniture for each area including style, quality, and interior finish materials. Designer will ensure the interior maintains a design that is both aesthetically pleasing and integrates client's existing furniture into the new scheme.

1.2. Project to be Lasertech site measured for accuracy and to establish AutoCAD as-built drawings including any equipment to be included within built-in millwork.

1.3. Determine requirements for furnishings and equipment including any equipment to be included within built-in millwork.

1.4. Obtain client's inventory list of existing furnishings (sizes, material, color, and pictures) to be included in the new space. Site verify as needed in conjunction with the room assignment plan that will be provided by the client.

Note: Client to provide CAD file for existing systems furniture layout.

1.5. Client to provide established budgetary guidelines to CDG for consideration during product specification.

2.   Design / Finishes

2.1. Using the information obtained in the Design Development phase, we will develop and present the interior space plan. The layout will take into consideration employee adjacencies and the most effective way to layout workspace based on job requirements and efficiency.

2.2. Again, using the information obtained in the Design Development phase, we will develop and present three conceptual design and color palette options for the project based on client requirements and budgetary guidelines. Materials to be specified within tenant improvement products provided by landlord or from similarly priced items from alternate manufacturers.

2.3. Specify all interior finishes including floor coverings, wall coverings, window treatments, laminates, paints, and stains. These recommendations shall be made with consideration given to ease of maintenance and durability.

2.4. Prepare and present the 2-D interior furniture plan for existing and new furniture as required.

2.5. Select and present furniture and fabric options for all new furnishings required.

2.6. Review architectural drawings to confirm integration of furniture layout with electrical plan and advise client of any adjustments required.

2.7. Prepare and present a typical workstation standard for systems furniture. Provide 2-D and 3-D plans for client review.

2.8. Prepare and present preliminary millwork elevations.

2.9. Before proceeding to Contract Documents, CDG, Inc. will obtain client approval on all plans and finishes.

3. Contract Documents

3.1. Prepare (1) set of color boards for the approved scheme. This board will be matted and framed in a basic metal frame.

Note: If desired, upgraded framing is available as a project expense.

3.2. Prepare an interior finish schedule for all specified interior-building finishes. This will include all locations of approved finish materials and design details.

3.3. Provide finalized furnishings selections with product pricing. Note: Separate client authorization will be required at that time to proceed with product procurement.

3.4. Provide installation plans for systems furniture noting all panel heights and components, electrical placement of duplex receptacles and base feeds / power pole locations and circuitry.

Note: Co-ordination of the systems furniture installation crew will be included as a service under separate contract with the purchase of systems furniture stations.

3.5. Prepare installation plans for the movers, detailing the locations of client's existing systems furniture and free-standing furniture, as well as detailed plans of any new furniture required. This includes printing individual room plans for use in proper furniture placement by the mover during relocation.

3.6. Prepare three specification binders detailing all finish specifications including product samples. Please note: One binder to be for the on-site use of the contractor, one for the clients' records, and one binder is to remain the property of CDG, Inc., as our permanent record of this project.

3.7. In conjunction with (list outsourced project architect here), CDG, Inc., will provide construction drawings to include standard architectural pages required for permit submittal. This includes the title page of project data, general notes, and index; the demolition plan, new construction plan, and keynotes; reflected ceiling plan; architectural details; door and window schedule; construction details, hardware schedule, and handicap notes.

Note: If available, client will provide vicinity map and site plan for accessible parking space configurations as required for building permit submittal. If client does not have this information available as an AutoCAD file, CDG can provide this plan as an additional service billed at our hourly rates.

3.8. CDG will coordinate providing base sheets to the client's designated general contractor and design build team for plumbing, mechanical, electrical, and fire protection. These plans will be bound together with the architectural pages for the convenience of the client during the bidding construction process.

4. Plan Check / Permitting

4.1. Preparation of plan check submittal sets.

4.2. Submittal of plans to Fire and Building Departments.

4.3. Plan check revisions and re-submittal as dictated by plan check comments. OR, (for City of Sacramento jurisdiction for specific project sites) . . . .

4.4. The project General Contractor will facilitate the city's Facilities Permit Program (FPP) including plan submittals to all review agencies.

4.5. Plan check corrections as dictated by plan check comments. Re-submit-tal to the city (if required) to be facilitated by the General Contractor.

5. Construction Administration / Move Coordination

5.1. Prior to construction commencing, CDG will respond to the client, the client's general contractor, and subs for pre-construction questions during the costing phase.

5.2. CDG, Inc., will facilitate construction administration on behalf of the client. Construction administration will include phone support and submittal review. This includes millwork and other disciplines as submitted by the general contractor.

5.3. Project coordination and job site observation services: Weekly construction meetings to coordinate timely completion of interiors with client and contractor. CDG will report weekly to the client on issues that need attention/action then follow through with that directive to the appropriate parties. During weekly site meetings, review and inspect the work to determine compliance with the documents and, if necessary, advise client of appropriate action regarding nonconforming work. Participate in the final "walk through" of the facility to confirm accuracy of all finishes and details.

5.4. CDG will interface directly with the movers to coordinate the installation of interior furnishings. CDG will coordinate the installation of the systems furniture with the IT/Telco subs, electrician, mover, and systems furniture installers. This typically requires a maximum of two team meetings, phone support, and site visits during installation as needed.

5.5. CDG will post the move plans at the new site. Using the furniture floor plan provided by CDG, the client will facilitate the tagging of furniture and contents to be relocated.

5.6. CDG will have a designer available on call during the major portion of your site relocation. Full time site supervision is not included.

5.7. CDG will assist the client with the recommendations for the final disposal of furnishings that are deemed no longer useful to the project. Costs for actual move and/or disposal are not included.

5.8. Assist in selection and placement of artwork, plants, and accessories.

6. Professional Fees and Conditions

6.1. Our fees are based upon our standard hourly rates for time required for the project.

Design Development, Design / Finishes (fixed fee) ... $_____

Contract Documents (fixed fee) .... $_____

Plan Check / Permitting (fixed fee) .... $_____

(NOTE: Municipality Plan Check & Permit Fees not included.)

Construction Administration - Service to be billed hourly per our rate schedule

Deposit Requested (50 percent at the onset of each phase listed above) .... $_____

(NOTE: At the onset of Construction Administration, a deposit will be required based on an estimate of the time needed for this phase. This deposit amount will be applied to the final invoice.)

6.2. Any additional time required to complete changes made to the plans and specifications after they have been approved, or to complete changes due to discrepancies in information provided by the client or client approved source, will be billed at our hourly rates.

6.3. Hourly rates as follows:

Principal Designer $225.00

Sr. Associate Designer/Certified Interior
Designer $185.00

Associate Designer $145.00

LASERtech CADD Plan Maintenance .... $ 95.00

CADD Drafting Technician .... $ 80.00

Design Assistant .... $ 80.00

6.4. In addition to our professional fee, we shall be reimbursed for project expenses at cost plus 15 percent, including all reproduction and related printing costs, supplies for presentation materials, and delivery services.

7. Terms and Conditions

7.1. Services required beyond the scope of services described in this agreement will be billed at our current hourly rates.

7.2. The Terms and Conditions set forth herein may be altered only upon approval of both the Client and Corporate Design Group, Inc., in writing.

7.3. If Corporate Design Group, Inc., retains an attorney to enforce its rights under this Agreement, Client agrees to pay reasonable attorney's fees and court costs.

7.4. Any extension of time for payment must be in writing and shall not release Client from any obligations under this Agreement.

7.5. Corporate Design Group, Inc., reserves the right to stop work on this project if our invoices are not paid within thirty (30) days of invoice.

7.6. If this proposal meets with your approval, it is understood that this letter constitutes our entire agreement and that no changes will be made except in writing, signed by Corporate Design Group, Inc., and the client.

7.7. This agreement may be terminated by you upon seven days written notice. In the event of termination, we shall be paid for services performed to date at the rates specified herein.

8. Additional Services Available

These services are not currently included in the proposal above but are available based upon our hourly rate schedule.

8.1. Detailed furniture specifications.

8.2. Development of the design concept for interior signage.

8.3. Perspective drawings and color renderings showing approved furnishings and finishes.

8.4. The following services are contingent upon the purchase of products through Corporate Design Group, Inc., and are provided at no charge.

CDG, Inc., will place orders directly with product manufacturers.

CDG, Inc., will track acknowledged shipping dates for all new furnishings.

CDG, Inc., will coordinate receiving and storage of all furnishings until time of installation as required. Furniture storage provided free for 30 days, if needed. Please note that you will find our furnishings prices to be competitive with other major office furniture dealers in the area.

To initiate the design process, your approval is required. Thank you for your consideration of this proposal. We look forward to working with you!

Sincerely,

Corporate Design Group, Inc.
Carol E. Parra, CEO, CID #0682
Certified Interior Designer - Approved Date

Carol and Corporate Design Group, Inc., have incorporated the very best aspects of good contract and client management. You will find your particular contract or letter of agreement will be slightly different from anyone else's because your business is different from everyone else's. By the examples cited, you will be able to construct your own contract for presentation to your client. Similar to a shopping list, you will pick and choose just the right elements to best demonstrate the services your firm offers.

A Residential Design Contract

A slightly different approach to contracts might just be the perfect solution for your firm. In this instance the contract includes items listed in other examples as additional charges, is shorter, and is possibly easier for the client to understand. I've also included a more concise and easier to understand procurement agreement. With these contracts the firm also has permission to pay invoices from an existing credit card on file with the design firm. You will see the procurement agreement is issued from a division of the parent company, Peninsula Interior Design, which offers a variation on how best to protect the assets of your firm.

Peninsula Interior Design

Dear Mr. and Mrs. John Friendly,

It was a pleasure meeting with you at our studio. We are pleased to submit this agreement for design consultation for your residence at Monterey Point.

Proposal for Interior Design Services

Scope of Service

A Non-refundable Retainer Fee will initiate the following:

1. Study of your furniture types and sizes to incorporate in the furniture plan drawn at ½" = 1'.
2. One meeting for all the selections of cabinets, counters, tile, and carpet.

71

3. Selection of paint colors and wall coverings as necessary.
4. Study of the lighting plan, making changes as needed, including revising the lighting plan and selecting fixtures and lighting as required.
5. Creation of window treatments and coverings as required.
6. Additional selections of furniture, art, and accessories as required.
7. Preparation of the presentation of design selections for your approval.
8. Printed quotations on all items to be ordered for your approval.
9. Installation of all items ordered from our offices.
10. Term of Contract: One year from date of signing

Payment:
A retainer of $10,000 will initiate your project. Fifty percent (50%) of this retainer will be refunded at the rate of 10 percent per invoice for items ordered with Peninsula Interior Design.

If purchases do not meet the full rebate amount, the balance will be retained by Peninsula Interior Design as compensation for services.

The following Terms and Conditions will be applicable to this contract:

1. Our retainer and fees will be billed against services, which include the following: telephone consultation time, planning, drafting, and AutoCad services, window measurement, window treatment installation, interior design project management, meeting with contractors, shopping, overseeing furniture delivery and travel time, one color selection meeting with builder/architect. You will be entitled to fifty (50) hours design and service time.

2. Printed quotations (Proposals) on all items to be ordered for your approval and deposit payments prior to any order being placed.

   Deposits:
   60 percent of total price for furniture, window treatments, art work, and accessories.
   60 percent for all labor.
   100 percent of any custom items such as furniture and built-ins.
   100 percent of any additional charges to include freight and/or storage.

3. Final payment is due at the time items are received in ware-house or items are ready for installation. No deliveries will be made without payment in full prior to delivery.

4. Title to merchandise will remain with Peninsula Interior Design until final payment is received.

5. All items are received and inspected prior to delivery. All deliveries will be overseen by our staff.

6. Custom orders are not returnable or refundable.

7. All proposals must be signed and dated at time of presentation, with notice of payment method for final balance due.

8. Any additional storage fees due to delays beyond the control of Peninsula Interior Design are the sole responsibility of the client and will be billed monthly.

9. Any past due invoices will be charged interest at the rate of 1.5 percent per month on the unpaid balance beginning on the 16th day after the due date of invoice.

10. Peninsula Interior Design shall be reimbursed for any costs, including reasonable attorney fees, incurred in the collection of delinquent money due under this contract.

11. Peninsula Interior Design offers an all-inclusive package and all drawings, schedules, and specifications as instruments of service are and remain the property of Peninsula Interior Design and its designers. The client may not use any Peninsula Interior Design drawings, schedules, or specifications for any project other than that contracted for without the written permission of, and the appropriate compensation to, Peninsula Interior Design. Any product or specification that is part of this presentation and is purchased elsewhere by the client is entitled to a compensation of twenty-five percent (25 percent) of the amount quoted by Peninsula Interior Design.

12. For advertising and promotion purposes Peninsula Interior Design will be allowed to photograph the project at various stages of development, use the photographs as it sees fit, and will ensure the privacy of the client and project location.

The client will also allow and permit Peninsula Interior Design to utilize the following credit card for all purchases as they arise. The client need not be on the premises.

CARD: # : _____

EXPIRY DATE: _____, 20_____

BILLING ADDRESS: _____ ZIP CODE: _____

As acceptance of this agreement please acknowledge and sign below. Please return the original to Peninsula Interior Design and retain the copy for your records.

Accepted: _____ Date: _____
    Mr. and Mrs. John Friendly

Accepted: _____ Date: _____
    Peninsula Interior Design

We are looking forward to helping you achieve a comfortable and exciting environment for your home.

A Purchase Agreement

Purchasing and Procurement

Byron Enterprises - A Division of Peninsula Interior Design, Inc. PURCHASING & PROCUREMENT. All products specified by Peninsula Interior Design, Inc., shall be purchased and procured through Byron Enterprises, a procurement division of Peninsula Interior Design, Inc. Byron Enterprises will act as your agent to purchase furniture, fabrics, accessories, lighting, and other items as specified. Purchasing agent duties will include specifications, ordering, tracking items, shipping and delivery, and billing. Byron Enterprises will bill all services and products to client. Byron Enterprises will apply discounts to products purchased through our offices whenever possible. The discounts will vary based upon individual suppliers. All freight, shipping, receiving, crating, storage, valuation protection, duties, and deliveries will incur a 20 percent handling fee. Final delivery charges will be billed to the client after delivery.

Deposits required to initiate the purchase of goods and services will be 75 percent of the total proposal. Deposits for fabrics, wall coverings, and floor coverings will be 100 percent of the proposal. In certain cases additional deposits may be due and payable prior to shipment.

Warranties and guarantees on all goods and services shall be only to the extent of those provided by the manufacturer, vendor, or suppliers. Byron Enterprises will not be liable for any errors, mistakes, or misrepresentations on the part of the vendor.

All prices are subject to change without notice. Byron Enterprises cannot guarantee that actual prices for merchandise and/or interior installation or other costs or services as presented to Client will not vary, either by item or in the aggregate, from any client proposals. Any omissions, price changes, or product changes will be brought to your attention immediately. Byron Enterprises reserves the right to correct all clerical errors such as addition, subtraction, and omission.

Balances due will be payable upon the presentation of the invoice. Any and all balances more than 30 days past due are subject to an interest charge of 1.5 percent per month. Byron Enterprises will be entitled to withhold delivery of any item ordered or the further performance of interior installations or any other services, should Client fail to make timely payments due to Byron Enterprises, Inc., or Peninsula Interior Design, Inc.

Client Approval. The client will be required to review and accept all proposals and/or contracts submitted by Byron Enterprises prior to any orders being placed. Acceptance of a proposal is constituted by a signature and the required deposit. The signed proposal and/or contract is an acknowledgement of the understanding and agreement to the terms of the proposal and/or contract. If authorization for deposit is placed by telephone, Byron Enterprises will mail the client a copy of the proposal and/or contract. If the deposit is a credit card purchase, the buyer authorizes the initial deposit to be charged immediately and the balance to be charged before delivery.

Cancelation. The proposal and/or contract cannot be canceled or modified after seventy-two (72) hours from the date it is signed and deposits received. There are no refunds on deposits and no returns after the seventy-two (72) hour period has elapsed; this applies to special orders as well as stock items. Damaged stock items cannot be returned once they have left the premises of Peninsula Interior Design. The proposal and/or contract may not be canceled due to delays in delivery caused by factors beyond Byron Enterprises control.

Signed _____ Date _____
Signed _____ Date _____

This particular part of the client management process is an important step toward fulfilling your obligations as an interior designer and professional business person. Many neophyte interior design professionals, myself included, started their businesses without a complete understanding of the complexities of the contract and letter of agreement processes. Take the time needed to acquaint yourself with the various aspects and ramifications of contracts. Once you have selected the type of agreement with which you are comfortable, get it into your system and use it. You will find the need to update your contract or agreement from time to time, but, in general, the contract or letter of agreement will remain the same from year to year. Now, with the signed agreement, you are ready to get to the heart and soul of interior design work. The first step, however, is not what you think. We're not ready for color and fabric selections, yet. Now is the time to consider the budget and how you and your client will arrive at numbers that will create the best possible design within the client's parameters.

CHAPTER FIVE

CREATING THE BUDGET

> "A billion here, a billion there, pretty soon it adds up to real money."
> — Senator Everett Dirksen (1896 – 1969)

Y ou've defined your optimum client, lured him to your office, met with him in his home, and walked away with a contract for services and procurement. Now all you have to do is create the beautiful interior both you and your client want to see. Not so fast. There is one very important step to take before you begin to pull together those wonderful ideas you have for the space. Contrary to what many people in the industry believe, budget creation is part of client and project management. By working with a professional interior designer, clients will be able to arrive at the best possible use of whatever financial limits they and you may set. Although your clients may have stated what they felt the budget should be, you must finalize the numbers, make a realistic estimate of what must be spent, and make selections based on your estimates. Without a realistic budget, you won't be able to begin the process of design and selection. Although the budget will not be set in stone, you must manage the numbers to stay within the budget parameters. Going over budget without first consulting the clients is unacceptable. They will make the ultimate decision as to how much will be spent on the project.

Determining the Budget

For budget purposes you won't simply be pulling numbers out of thin air. Your budget specifications will be based on what will be needed to complete the project within the confines of the scope of the project. During the budget-making process you will also start making preliminary selections for the space. Once you have established what you need, the budget process can move forward. There are a number of ways to begin and you will decide what is right for your client. Kathryn Long, ASID, in Asheville, North Carolina, shows current clients what former clients spent on similar projects. She doesn't give away names but does show how certain choices will affect the overall amount of money that will have to be spent to achieve the same level of finish and style. This gives her clients a better understanding of how much they will have to spend to create the space they want. You will still be responsible for writing up the budget, but at least there will be a figure with which to work. The same outcome could be achieved by using photos of recently completed projects.

Some designers have created small workbooks, which include generic types of furniture, fabrics, and finishes, to give a range of pricing to achieve a budget figure. Whatever you decide, you don't want to simply throw a dollar amount at your clients and expect them to placidly agree. Nor is the "shotgun" approach to budget creation the best way to achieve financial success for your firm. Budgets based on nothing more than your gut feelings often have a way of getting larger as the project progresses, so it's best to start with a realistic figure. As you expand and flesh out the budget, it becomes easier to understand how and where the money will be spent. Most budgets ultimately include specific pricing for specific pieces and finishes in the space. Something similar to a line item budget is what will be needed.

By the Numbers

It's not as hard as it might seem to create a line item budget. Take a look at the number and types of pieces you are going to need for the space. If its multiple spaces, create smaller budgets for each space then combine them all for the larger budget number. By starting with the final budget figure and deducting the items you choose as you go along, the number will finally reach zero. If you've included everything you want for the space, it becomes a balanced budget. If not, you will reselect, subtract items, or reduce the number of multiple items selected until you balance the needs of the project against the needs of the budget. For a very large project this can take hours of research, even though you may have a very clear idea of what is needed for a specific space. I never, and I mean never, go over the budget figure agreed upon with the client during the interview phase. I will, during the presentation, show options for specific pieces, and the client will decide whether or not to increase the budget. At this point my job is to balance the budget, and I make sure during discussions that it is a realistic dollar figure for the size and style of the proposed project.

My partner, Robert, and I recently completed the renovation of a 4,550-square-foot home in a local golf resort. The clients had been referred to us by their real estate agent and consulted us before hiring a builder or contractor. We helped define the scope of the project, select the builder, and create the budget for the proposed work. We charged for our time while working to create the budget, and our contractor worked through our office to make sure we covered all the necessary items for completion. In the beginning we included exterior changes that were ultimately dropped from the project. We realized early on that the kitchen, which the client thought might work as is, would need a complete makeover. The need for the new kitchen created a situation in which the budget would have to go up without deleting some other aspect of the project. At this point we reviewed the choices that had already been selected and approved. Among them was a redesign and build of a series of four bay windows, which included the laying of new foundation slabs for each window. The redesign called for the base of each window to be clad to match the exterior of the home. The cost was about $12,000 per window for a total of just over $48,000. We decided, along with the client, to eliminate the redesign and build out of the bay windows and leave them as they were. The choice to remove the proposed exterior changes reflected the need for a newer kitchen. That's how budgets work.

As we worked through the needs of the interior we decided to remove one fireplace in a very small room and create another in the master bedroom. We opened a wall between the kitchen and dining room to create vista views overlooking the golf course for both spaces and decided to create a space for a wine cooler that included a small refrigerator. Within seven working days I was prepared to present a proposed budget to the clients.

One from Column A, One from Column B

We decided to present two levels of finish and cost and let the client choose one or mix and match. The master budget included demolition of the inside of the house to the studs where needed and a complete redo of the interiors. There was very little exterior work, but the interior was gutted. Our builder presented a proposed budget, and we presented our interior suggestions for budget approval. I hadn't selected specific items at this point but knew, from experience, where the budget needed to be for the finish and style the client wanted for the project. I created the written budget to show the pricing options and the range in which the budget might fall. I thought about what would be needed and added a little bit at the end to cover those unforeseen items all clients usually want or feel they need. The process is a little like creating a shopping list.

In the example budget below, the items listed can be expanded or changed as needed for your particular project. The essence of a budget is to see where money will be spent and to ascertain whether or not changes can be made and how they might affect the overall total. Of course, you could produce this on an Excel spread sheet or using your accounting and budgeting software, but the most important thing is to come up with a realistic spread of costs that the client is comfortable with and that will help you maintain control of the budget.

HALE-WILLIAMS INTERIOR DESIGN

RE: Mr. and Mrs. Frederick Lawton

Preliminary Budget   Furnishings & Finishes   June 16, 2009

Entry

New Fixture	$1,500	$4,000

Living Room

Sofa, leather	$8,500	$15,500
Chairs (4)	$14,000	$30,000
Chairs (2), swivel	$9,300	$11,300
Tables–cocktail (1), side (2), sofa (1), tea (1)	$5,000	$9,500
Console	$2,000	$4,000
Side chairs (2)	$2,500	$5,000
Lamps–floor (2), table (4 to 6)	$3,000	$5,000
Sconces (4)	$1,000	$2,000
Drapery	$8,000	$17,000
Rugs	$20,000	$30,000
	$73,300	$129,300

Dining Room

Table	$3,500	$6,000
Chairs (8)	$4,000	$8,000
Drapery	$3,000	$6,000
Rug	$4,000	$12,000
	$14,500	$32,000

Kitchen

Bar stools (4)	$3,200	$7,000
Window seat cushions	$1,500	$3,000
Lighting	$750	$1,500
Drapery	$2,000	$4,000
Shoji screen	$2,500	$5,000
	$9,950	$20,500

Family Room

Recliner chairs (2) or chairs and ottomans (2)	$4,000	$15,000
Game/high-low table and chairs (4)	$4,500	$8,000
Lighting	$1,500	$3,700
TV furniture	$1,500	$5,000
Drapery	$3,000	$5,000
Carpet (Approx. 40 sq. yds)	$3,000	$3,300
	$17,500	$40,000

Hallway

Carpet (Approx. 26 sq. yds)	$1,950	$2,500

Powder Room

Wall covering (Approx. 6 rolls plus installation)	$1,500	$2,000
Lighting	$450	$1,000
	$1,950	$3,000

Mrs. Lawton's Office

Desk, chair, etc.	$3,500	$9,500
Lighting	$1,500	$2,500

Drapery	$1,500	$4,000
Carpet (Approx. 12 sq. yds)	$900	$1,000
	$7,400	$17,000

Guest Bedroom

Bed, night stands, dresser or chest	$6,500	$12,000
Bedding	$1,500	$5,500
Lighting	$1,000	$3,000
Drapery	$2,000	$4,000
Carpet (Approx. 29 sq. yds)	$2,200	$2,500
	$13,200	$25,000

Mr. Lawton's Office

Window treatment	$2,500	$5,500
Carpet (Approx. 25 sq. yds)	$2,500	$5,000
Desk chair and lounge chair	$4,000	$10,000
Lighting	$1,000	$3,500
	$10,000	$24,000

Guest Bath

Window treatment	$750	$2,500

Master Bedroom

Bed, night stands, chest	$6,500	$14,500
Bedding	$1,500	$5,500
Chairs (2), ottoman (1)	$5,000	$12,000
Lighting	$1,500	$6,500

Drapery	$4,500	$9,500
Carpet (Approx. 75 sq. yds)	$7,300	$8,500
	$26,300	$56,500
Master Bath		
Window treatment	$1,000	$2,500
Totals		
Entry	$1,500	$4,000
Living Room	$73,300	$129,300
Dining Room	$14,500	$32,000
Kitchen	$9,950	$20,500
Family Room	$17,500	$40,000
Hallway	$1,950	$2,500
Powder Room	$1,950	$3,000
Mrs. Lawton's Office	$7,400	$17,000
Guest Bedroom	$13,200	$25,000
Mr. Lawton's Office	$10,000	$24,000
Guest Bath	$750	$2,500
Master Bedroom	$26,300	$56,500
Master Bath	$1,000	$2,500
	$179,300	$358,800
Shades–as quoted	$19,631	$19,631
"Can't live without" items, additional accessories, plants, add-ons, and other items @ 10 percent of budget	$20,000	$37,900
	$218,931	$416,331

CREATING THE BUDGET

This simple line item budget enabled us to work with the client and deduct and add items as specific selections occurred. All of us had a copy with which to work during the budget meeting, and I made updated copies before the clients left after the meeting. Ultimately, the clients decided to settle on a dollar figure of $325,000 for our part of the project. Would I have been able to guess that's where they would end up for the budget? Probably. As so often happens when given a choice, clients tend to go for the middle ground. They don't want to appear cheap, yet don't want to seem profligate. If I actually wanted the larger sale should I have skewed the figures up to create a new center? No, that wasn't what I wanted to do. The presented budget was organized around what I knew the pricing would probably be and what I believed the client would ultimately want to spend. I believe we actually arrived at a realistic budget for the project and the needs of the client. I was happy, as were they. As you gain more experience in budget creation and management you will find that it becomes easier, and your sense of how much it will ultimately cost will become sharper.

Another Perspective

Diana S. Walker, ASID, owns and operates her eponymous interior design firm in Houston, Texas, and has a wealth of experience in dealing with budget creation and managing clients. Her perspective on budget preparation incorporates old and new techniques that relate to the demands of today's interior designers, builders, and contractors.

"When I worked for a twenty-person interior design firm, one of my assignments from the firm's owner was to put together a book of budgets and information about the quality of the product lines we worked with at our firm. It was an arduous task that involved utilizing the best sourcing information we had from jobs in progress and resource room price sheets. Each product was dissected within three areas: high, mid-range, and basic. Interns gained valuable experience helping our firm do canvassing for costs and information. I recently came upon this eighteen-year-old binder and was surprised how simplistic it was in light of what we use today.

What this did for the entire professional firm was enable anyone in our firm to be more accurate when putting together a project, whether high-end, medium, or basic, and to assign a projected cost for each item. My team had organized a large range of products from which to pull. This was before we had computers and the Internet to search for information, yet we were able to capture something that was tangible and helped tremendously. We used a handful of standard trades, but our direct purchase was broad and we had a diverse group of designers with many experiences and important jobs. We went into any budget negotiation confident in our decisions because we had done our homework.

With the use of Excel spread sheets and computers, budget organization is far simpler today than it once was, but there are still a number of things to be aware of before submitting a proposed budget to clients.

Budgets routinely change from the time of the initial proposal to the time final selections are made. Your communication with clients is critical to determining what they intend to spend. Often a client will make his or her decision only after all the costs are factored into the equation. There are a few tips I would suggest all interior designers employ when creating a budget for clients.

Information Is Power

Begin by gathering accurate data as you work on projects and gain more knowledge about actual costs for each item or service. I keep all copies of my initial budgets for jobs. During and after the project I compare these initial budgets to the actual costs for the project. I ask for complete job reports from my accountant and my typical time billings for each job. These are kept in a binder in my filing cabinet, so when I must come up with something quickly I have the information readily at hand. I also keep a copy of the construction budgets for each job, as these are often set too low. When cost issues arise, I can speak to the problem with knowledge and accurate information.

Builders have told me they like having someone from my staff work with them to ascertain accurate and up-to-date costs and delivery issues. When discrepancies arise, knowing what the construction budget was originally intended to be, and was ultimately found to be insufficient, enables you to confidently address other clients in the same position on future jobs. Reading a builder's construction allowance budget can also be misleading. Make time to sit down with the builder and the client to discuss the budget and clarify which areas include labor, freight/delivery, and whether or not sales tax is included. At this time you will want to show how the builders allowance and the budget work together–or don't. If the builder has used budget numbers that do not reflect the level of finish, style, or design the client wants for the project, now is the time to make changes to the building budget. This was something I failed to do only once.

Time Is Money

Be sure to value your time properly when preparing a budget. You are giving a client your knowledge and expertise. You will find more and more clients need your input to arrive at a fair and accurate budget. The last three prospects I interviewed asked for my assistance in creating a budget.

Suggest to your clients that they decide on some contingency amount above the ultimate budget total and of which you will not be informed. When something they really want is more expensive than budgeted, they can take the money from the contingency account. I have actually started putting a contingency line item amount, a percentage of twelve percent to fifteen percent, within each budget area to be used for increased freight, extra charges for things that come up during the final weeks before installation, or that one item the client decides he or she simply can't live without.

I personally prepare separate budgets for furnishings, lighting, wall coverings, window treatments, art and accessories, bedding, and other soft goods. This way I know I have included everything needed. I include all custom fabricated items that might normally be handled on a builder's budget.

An Estimated Budget

Until an item is purchased and installed, label everything *estimated* budget figures and date the budget so you know what the latest and most accurate figures are. I had a designer friend who had an entire house worth of custom furnishings destroyed in a tractor-trailer accident one week before installation. Because she had accurate budget and purchase figures she was ultimately able to resolve the insurance claim, though at the time the process was grueling and time consuming.

People don't equate "net cost" with "net cost to a designer." Clients want to know how much, exactly, they will pay for an item without any hidden costs. I have always worked with price transparency, showing my markup, but it means I have to take time to explain what the terminology means to clients and what they ultimately will pay. Some designers do not show their markup as a separate line item. I have found both ways—showing markup separately or not—helpful, depending on the client and the job.

Prepare sufficiently for all discussions of budgets, finances, and billings. Don't ever submit something you don't fully understand. You should expect questions about the process by which you arrived at the budget figures and how it will all work within the allowance for the purchases. As with all processes within your office, strict adherence to detail for budgets will enhance your position to your client and ultimately make your job easier."

Easy Access

The accumulation of information for budget purposes can be time consuming. Budget preparation is part of the design process and you should include the cost of its preparation in your retainer or design fee. A current library will help make the process easier and less time consuming for you and your client. Your library should include the catalogues and samples from firms that keep an updated price list available either online or in printed form and to which you have instant access. Waiting around for days on end for a vendor or showroom to get back to you with pricing is unacceptable when putting together a budget.

If at all possible, maintain open accounts with those firms and keep up to date with their latest offerings or presentations. The men and women who work with you to create drapery, measure and install carpeting and wall coverings, and create custom cabinets or furniture should also be aware of your need for prompt and accurate quotes. I often use the floor plan to estimate the amount of carpet or wall covering the space will need and to extrapolate a quote for preliminary budget figures. Knowing the usual charges for carpet padding and installation and an estimated per roll pricing for wall covering helps me move the process along until the mechanic is able to get back to me with a quote. Once I receive a more accurate quote, I substitute the figures from the mechanic for my initial figures. All of these prices and estimated quantities are the first step in creating a precise and usable budget for your client.

The "Blue Sheet"

As you receive quotes from various sources, incorporate them into your budget worksheet. I use plain lined paper for rough estimates for client costs. On this rough sheet I insert cost estimates from the various sources for whatever I am pricing. For drapery there will be a list of the items needed to complete the window covering. I insert the cost of fabric, trim, lining and interlining, fabrication, hardware, and installation. If I am also pricing shades or blinds for the same window, those prices are inserted. I include our markup in the estimate and add the whole thing up for a total "presented price." Once I'm sure I have the information for a particular item I add it to what is referred to in our office as a "blue sheet." The name is derived from the color of the paper on which we print the worksheet form. The color allows me or anyone else in the office to immediately identify the piece as a complete or final budget estimate for presentation to the client, but not to be used for the final quote for proposal preparation. Once the client signs off on an item or piece for the project we then move it over to proposal preparation. This is the last stop before the client is presented with the proposal and we collect the deposit to begin ordering or fabrication. The rough worksheet, blue sheet, and a copy of the proposal will eventually go into the client file or notebook. The paper trail is very important to client and project management and will be very helpful should there be any questions regarding pricing for a specific item.

The Contractor Myth

Now let's have a word about builders and contractors. They offer a wide range of services that include labor priced at man-hours, fixtures and fittings not usually supplied by an interior designer, and selections of trims and woodwork that require a knowledge of design styles and periods. Trying to get a quote from them is quite often like pulling teeth. The task becomes laborious and time consuming. As so often happens, they would much more prefer to quote in terms of time and materials. That's fine but it doesn't give anyone a clear idea of how much total construction costs can be. I ask my contractor to create a figure based on what we anticipate needing. This particular quote will be labeled as preliminary and it is understood that the pricing may change. This is time consuming for the builder who quite often is not compensated for his or her services when it comes to quotes for proposed work. I have, for certain projects, asked clients to pay a small fee for comprehensive quotes. Once I explain the detail to which the builder will go for the quotes, they have no problem paying a small fee. Once the builder knows he's to be paid for the quote it becomes far easier to produce a legitimate quote for the proposed services. I also explain to builders that clients will feel more inclined to use their services once they've paid a fee for a more refined quote. The client will feel as if the builder has become a part of the team already.

The Fifty-Dollar Toilet

Contractors and builders are notorious for under-pricing the items that will be included in the construction of new or renovated spaces. For example, it is absurd to estimate $5.00 a square foot for procurement and installation of stone flooring in a home or renovation for anything but the most modest of residences. The clients with whom most of us deal will be looking for flooring that is far more expensive. I have actually seen quotes from builders for bathroom fixtures that underestimated true costs by thousands of dollars. I once saw a quote from a builder of fifty dollars as the budget estimate for a toilet in a guest bath. When I asked about the discrepancy between that figure and the actual cost of a good toilet I was told it was based on the budget and the need to cut costs somewhere. That's fine, but there isn't anything like a fifty-dollar toilet out there.

So, if the builder isn't honest enough to explain to his client, and yours, that the budget isn't large enough, there will be problems. I once worked with clients who had already hired their builder and agreed upon a quote of $300 a square foot for construction. The clients explained that was the budget they set based on what they had paid for a commercial building the same builder had constructed for them two years before. In our area the actual cost for luxury residential construction is nearer to $400 to $450 per square foot. As I tried to explain the reality of costs to the client and the huge difference between commercial and residential construction costs, I once again wondered why the builder would even sign that contract.

Ultimately the clients and I took a look at the builder's quote and made adjustments as needed. We presented our new budget totals to the builder and asked him to adjust his pricing accordingly. He was hesitant until we explained that we understood why the costs would rise and we would not ask for more quotes from other builders. The final cost for the construction phase of the project was just over $412 per square foot and we had projected $427. The builder later told me he had learned a valuable lesson for future quotes on the type of residential work we were doing. The project moved forward with very few change orders and the clients were happy because there weren't any shocking surprises once the construction phase began. Unless you have very good working relationships with contractors or builders, take a careful look at their quotes before you suggest that a client move forward on a project. By underestimating and manipulating the pricing of items for the project, the builder gives an unrealistic budget figure for the proposed work. A professional interior designer must be vigilant when working with unknown builders or contractors. Their inaccurate pricing could bring the whole project to a halt until the client is fully aware of the actual cost of items included in the builder's quote.

The Budget Meeting

Once you are happy with the amount of information you have accumulated, set a time for your clients to come into the office for a budget meeting. I usually divide this meeting into a builder/contractor meeting and an interior selection meeting. Both are budget meetings, but each has different parameters. The builder/contractor meeting might include that person. Like any other meeting you have with your clients, this meeting should include a short agenda and specific items to be discussed.

Budget Meeting: Mr. and Mrs. Frederick Lawton, June 30, 2009, 1:30 – 3:00 p.m.

- **Review items from budget lists**
- **Preliminary selections for budget**
- **Client sign-off for initial budget totals**

I plan for this meeting, like most other meetings, to last no more than ninety minutes. Although there will be preliminary furnishing selections, the final choices have yet to be made. This meeting is focused on the budget total and includes an overview of selections, without specifics. Your expertise as a client manager will come into play as you present the numbers and your preliminary thoughts on selections. Don't let the clients become preoccupied with the minutia of specific items within the overall budget. If you are including a complete remodel of the kitchen keep the conversation focused on the overall quality and style desired and not the specific pull that might be used on the doors. If you have decided on a sofa for the living room don't get distracted by trying to decide exactly what trim will be used for the throw pillows. You are painting with a much broader brush for this meeting—details will come during later presentations.

During the preparation for this meeting you will have spent a lot of time working with architectural drawings, finish schedules, and possibly lighting plans. Be sure to separate the items of furnishings your firm will supply from those items that will be included in the construction and remodeling phase of the project by the contractor or builder. As discussed earlier, this line item budget is just that: lines and lines of budget proposals. During this process you might have to make an occasional SWAG (Sophisticated Wild-Assed Guess). Your SWAGs will be based on your knowledge of pricing, cost, and item availability. For this preliminary budget you will not be able to have firm quotes for each item you are about to discuss, but don't, on the other hand, simply try to pull a number out of the sky. Keep your budget estimates realistic and within reason. The last thing you want is to underestimate what an item might cost based on unreliable information.

How Budgets Affect Your Business

Once you have the budget in your computer and on paper, it is easy to make changes as they occur, and they will occur. You and the client will decide to add components to the original scope of the project or deduct trim for a particular set of draperies. Management of the budget becomes far easier once you have it in your excel program. With excel or any other type of accounting and management software, immediate updates are easy and allow you and your client instant access to precise dollar figures for specific items. The client budget process also affects your business' bottom line. It becomes an important part of your financial projections and gives you a much better idea of future cash flow. A realistic client project budget helps to establish projections that will help you create internal budgets important to forecasting monetary needs.

Although many designers have little or no interest in cash flow and receivables, they are an important factor in client and project management. Without a clear understanding of the importance of a budget, a designer is unable to work in a professional and ethical manner. Precise figures, after all, help keep everyone abreast of the project and maintain equilibrium between client and interior designer. Only with a complete budget are you able to move ahead with preparing an intelligent and comprehensive final presentation for your client.

CHAPTER SIX

CLIENT COMMUNICATION AND CONTACT

" The most important thing in communication is
to hear what isn't being said. "
— Peter Drucker (1909 – 2005)

There are times when we all feel our clients don't hear what we're saying and don't understand what we've already told them. Communication is so important to client and project management. I know you've heard it so many times before that you will think I am just passing along another cliché. If so, you couldn't be further from the truth. Communication is one of the most important skills needed as you pursue your career as a professional interior designer. Direct contact is what will set the tone for the professional management of your client and the project. How and when you manage that contact is the essence of honing your skills as an adept and talented manager. It is not just your message that is important. What they want and need to tell you quite often defines whether or not a project is as successful as it could be. Communication has a certain style and rhythm based on the particular type being used. Talking one on one is far different from a formal written letter. Understanding the differences between various types of communication helps you control the tenor and outcome of each transaction. This is a two-way street and you better be on the right side to ensure you hear from your client in a timely and efficient manner. You will want to constantly communicate the status of the project to keep the client engaged and focused on what decisions will need to be made over the coming weeks or months. Professional communication management is yet another important aspect of your job not covered in Interior Design 101.

How you handle the challenge and what tools you employ to communicate with clients is vital to the success of the project.

Keep in Touch

Effective communication is also a part of your marketing and promotion campaign. Although far more subtle than advertising and direct mail marketing, your professional handling of client communication will enhance the overall stature of your firm in the eyes of your clients. As with so many aspects of client and project management, your professionalism is defined by how you handle this part of the job. The right stationery and proper use of the written word will also contribute to your branding and positioning endeavors.

Understanding the benefits improved interaction skills will bring to your business is important. Why, exactly, do you contact your client? How do you contact your client? Is your style of communication clear and concise? These are important questions, and a thoughtful review of the various types of communication will help you organize your efforts. Improved communication skills will help you and your firm better understand your clients' goals and what they want from the proposed project. These skills will also help you reduce wasted effort when preparing design proposals and presentations. This all brings increased value to your clients. They will feel more secure in your management skills and your ability to create the interiors they want for a specific project.

Setting an Agenda

There are several typical types of contact you and your firm will have with a client over the course of a project. The most important are meetings and discussions. This one-on-one communication will define your style as a manager. When you bring your clients and your design team together, you should know what you would like to accomplish during the meeting and how long you believe the meeting should last. An agenda would be helpful, but a simple outline of the objectives will suffice. I don't suggest you adhere strictly to a printed form but try to keep the meeting moving forward as much as possible. I suggest keeping this type of meeting to around ninety minutes. Most people lose focus if meetings last much longer than that.

Meetings can be time consuming and boring unless everyone understands the importance of the work at hand. Most often these meetings are for presenting and reviewing design ideas and concepts. Open each meeting with a short review of what will be covered in the upcoming discussions. Once you've established the subject or subjects to be covered, move directly to the subject of the meeting. Start the presentation, begin to explain the electrical plan or focus on the elevations to be viewed. Explain in detail what you want the client to understand about the subjects of this particular meeting. Answer any questions that might arise and conclude the meeting in a timely manner. Don't get waylaid by extraneous subjects and unrelated questions. Avoid the temptation to allow anyone to detour down an unproductive path. When you see this happening simply suggest in a mild voice that you all "move on." That way you maintain focus on the matter at hand and control of your client and the meeting. There are more details on this subject in chapter 8. Suffice it to say, you will want to ensure everyone leaves the meeting with a complete understanding of what took place and without any lingering questions.

Other types of face-to-face meetings might involve fine-tuning the budget, selection follow-up, reselection, or continued design presentations. Each of these should have the same parameters as all one-on-one meetings and be organized to accomplish defined goals. In all of these meetings there will be some give and take of ideas and philosophies, and you will strive to ensure the stated goals are achieved. Good client and project management requires you to keep everyone on track without giving up a true sense of collaboration. Your clients need to feel a part of the project and decision-making process. Don't ignore their questions and make sure they feel comfortable with the decisions being made at each of these different types of meetings. It is also a good idea to summarize the outcome of each meeting in written form and distribute it to the clients and design team members involved in the project. Your team will also have particular action items that arise from this meeting, to which they should attend as needed. Updates on the status of those tasks should be included in your weekly staff meetings.

Who's Calling, Please?

The next most prevalent type of contact is telephone calls. These can be more problematic, because they happen without a pre-set time and generally intrude into your busy schedule. Although many clients will call whenever they want, most firms will take a message and have you or the specified designer return the call at a more convenient time. By returning the call later rather than taking it on the spot, you and your team are able to organize your thoughts and bring together any supporting material, if necessary, to keep the call focused on a defined topic. Timing is also important, and with preparation your team is able to manage the call and keep the length of time it takes to a minimum. Depending on the type of call there may be additional action needed to satisfy the client. That will be up to you and your design team to define, organize, and implement. When returning calls, always ask clients if it's a good time to talk. You want them to be focused on the answers you have for the questions they asked. As you address each component of the phone call, take notes and ensure the client is satisfied with the solutions suggested. This type of call is often followed by an e-mail summarizing the call and outlining what you and your firm will do to arrive at the agreed-upon solutions.

E-mail

The easiest type of communication by far is e-mail. Generally the client does not expect an immediate answer, so you are able to organize your thoughts for a response. You should use e-mail just like any other communication tool. Maintain a precise style and structure to ensure clear and concise replies. Although not as formal as written communication, e-mails are also still text-based. With that in mind, I usually structure my e-mails just like a letter. I start with a salutation of some sort and always include a closing remark. This helps maintain an air of professionalism. I don't use contractions such as "R U OK" nor do I add little notes like "LOL," all of which make the e-mail read more like a text message—not great for client relations and very unprofessional. As with all types of written communication, keep copies of all e-mail correspondence. Copies will help you resolve any questions that might arise from actions taken in response to specific e-mails.

Attachments to e-mails help expand the scope of the message and add to the overall effectiveness of your communication. Photographs, tear sheets, and color renderings can all be attached to most e-mails you send. As a preliminary to any selection meetings, e-mail communication reminds the client of what has already been seen, what you might suggest as an alternate solution, or what might replace an item that is no longer available. The client won't feel rushed to make a decision and will come to the meeting more prepared to move forward.

Another aspect of project and client management is how you answer e-mails and when you read them. Keeping your e-mail alarm on all the time can interfere with your ongoing duties as chief executive officer of your business and distract you from other tasks. One of the best time management solutions is to devote a specific time of day to reading and answering e-mails. You will also find that many e-mails can be handled by members of your staff. Always forward those e-mails as soon as you've read them. For e-mails you must answer yourself, wait until you have the time to organize your thoughts or do the research necessary to answer in a complete manner. Simply reply that you will need some time to formulate an answer and you will get back to the client within twenty-four hours. Never allow e-mails to sit in your inbox without some sort of reply. It's bad manners and your client will become annoyed.

You will also find that communication between you and your staff will probably be most efficient through e-mails and text messages. These types of communication will be less formal and more abbreviated, though you still need to include all necessary facts and information. Don't, for the sake of brevity, reduce any message to the point that it becomes unintelligible or vague. It is critical that the message makes it clear to everyone that what is being conveyed is important.

A Stationery Package

Written communication is still one of the most persuasive and important ways of communicating with your clients. This, of course, includes contracts, proposals, invoices, and any other business forms needed to move a project forward. You will have already defined what type of stationery your firm will use—this will include any forms or contracts used for projects. These are the nuts and bolts of contact with your client and you want the style of the stationery pieces to define and enhance your firm's professional stature. The stationery should be simple and clean with your company's logo, if you so choose, as well as a way for the client to contact you in reply. Don't print your own stationery from a computer software program onto cheap white paper. Have business stationery printed locally and use your creative talents to develop stationery that is elegant, tasteful, and reflects you and your business. Business stationery with floral icons, kittens, or puppies sends a message to your client that may not be the one you intend. Keep it simple. You are, after all, doing business here.

Most firms maintain an image with their stationery that is unified and simple. Each envelope, letterhead, invoice, note, or proposal, also known as collateral material, has the same look as all the others. The consistency is what's important here. Any time your firm sends out written communication, where it's from is immediately evident to the client. That is the goal of having a uniform look for your stationery. You don't want clients setting aside your very important message because they didn't recognize the stationery.

As a means of doing business, written communication is designed to impart information in a precise and clear way. When it comes to invoices, we print them all on our company stationery. The forms that come from QuickBooks or other management software simply don't have the sophisticated look or feel of elegant and professional stationery nor the business-like appeal of a service invoice. We feel the more formal approach lends a more professional style to our corporate communication and image. By all means make sure any mathematics included in the letter or invoice has been double checked for accuracy. You don't want a mistake at this point. As the invoice is prepared, double check that all deposits paid have been applied to the balance due and any credits due or debits to be applied have appeared on the statement.

For contracts, the corporate stationery is used for the cover letter and, if used, the letter of agreement. You may decide to use a secondary letter-head page that doesn't have the full-blown corporate image embossed at the top but has the same color, feel, and look of the more impressive cover letterhead. The creation and organization of all your collateral material sets the tone of the firm and ensures your client appreciates the very high standards you set for your designs and your business.

Just a Little Note

We have always included in our stationery line-up a note card and return envelope that includes the same look as the other stationery we use. These note cards are used as thank you notes, update notes, and anything we think is appropriate for more informal contact. We also always handwrite this type of note. It might be used to congratulate a client on a birthday, child's graduation, or some other event. I usually don't get overly sentimental with this note and try to keep it under about fifty words. It's a way of touching base with clients and it produces the most comments from our clients. Why? Because no one sends out thank you notes anymore.

When was the last time you got a beautiful handwritten note from anyone? Clients are impressed you remembered a particular occasion and even more impressed that you actually took the time to send a handwritten note. If you feel your handwriting isn't up to snuff then have someone in your office write the note from your dictation. You, or the appropriate individual, should always personally sign these notes whether dictated or written by your own hand. Either way, this type of communication will go far in elevating your status in your clients' eyes.

Calling cards, like the rest of your stationery, should be consistent with the image you project as a firm. Keep the card simple. It should be a standard size that will fit easily into someone's hand and pocket. Oversized, square, or odd-shaped cards tend to be discarded as quickly as possible. Cards that have an overabundance of colors, images, or patterns are more difficult to read and, therefore, also discarded as soon as possible.

Communication, of course, is not a one-way street. As with telephone calls, there are times when your clients will want to contact you with specific questions, ideas, or thoughts on the project. Understanding what, exactly, clients are saying when they reach out to you is important. Missing the true intent of a telephone call or short, written note from a client could cause you to lose the confidence of that client. Your ability to listen, correctly interpret, and act upon the input from clients is essential to good client and project management. With that in mind there are a few other communication tools I would suggest you add to your tool belt. One of the most informative and interesting is the survey. This feedback tool has become one of the most effective ways in which your firm can track successes and eliminate expensive mistakes for clients and projects.

Give and Take

Mike Phillips is a Professional Member of AIA (The American Institute of Architects), a Professional Member IIDA (International Interior Design Association), and a registered interior designer in North Carolina. Mike is also the founder and president of DesignFacilitator.com, the design industry's first interactive online tool for design firms to use in surveys and information collection. Mike's thoughts help define the need for this very powerful client management tool.

"Architects, engineers, and interior designers are typically listed in survey.com's Top 10 Most Respected Professions in the United States. We add aesthetic beauty to the environments in which people live and, just as importantly, are hired to solve clients' problems. We are most effective when we clearly understand those problems, but our clients often present us with limited information. To compound the difficulty, the client's information is typically project-oriented rather than problem-oriented. For example, clients may show a space they 'like,' but are unable to put into words why they like it. Project-oriented information like this can be misleading and create huge gaps in our understanding of the client's needs and preferences. While you can gain some direction from this information, beginning a design based only on this type of input is often perilous in terms of wasting time and false starts.

Gathering Information

In order to communicate most effectively with your clients, the ability to assemble problem-oriented information is critical. Collecting problem-oriented information from your clients allows them to tell you what problems they have, how solutions will improve their lives, and why they need your help. This better informs designers as to the nature of the clients' problems and helps define the most constructive processes for creating solutions. With this information, designers are more efficient in arriving at the solution quickly. Problem-oriented information reduces wasted time and effort on the designer's part, which often helps increase your project profitability.

Some designers may argue that clients are responsible for communicating all pertinent information to their designer and to do so in a manner that allows the designer a complete understanding of the project. Most designers, however, who take that position, are frustrated at the lack of success with their clients. Conversely, a more proactive designer who takes the lead in collecting information and truly understanding their clients is likely to have a growing list of successful projects and satisfied clients.

In 2005, the Construction Specifications Institute sponsored a study in which builders and clients were asked to identify the biggest problem they had with designers. With remarkable consistency the answer given was WASTE. They felt designers did not understand their needs sufficiently and did not stay on track to create an appropriate solution in a practical amount of time. Let me repeat: *Clients and builders felt that designers did not understand their needs sufficiently and did not stay on track to create an appropriate solution in a practical amount of time.*

Just as a dentist might tell you that you only need to take care of the teeth you want to keep, clearly you only need to take the lead and communicate well to the clients with whom you wish to have a successful project. Every project counts, and designer-driven, problem-oriented communication and a broad understanding of every client are essential to a designer's success.

Given the paramount importance of understanding your client, it may indeed seem surprising to hear an experienced designer admit that there is never enough time to completely understand his or her clients' needs before starting work on solving their problems and designing their projects. While challenging, this situation exists because of the enormous amount of relevant information the client possesses. If designers waited until all the pertinent client information was obtained, the design work would never begin. And, if the designer takes too long to start designing, he or she will probably be fired. This is the designer's quandary but there is a surprisingly simple solution.

Where to Begin

The most efficient and effective manner in which most projects should proceed is:

- Gathering initial information from clients
- Designing an initial response
- Presenting a response to client
- Gathering feedback from client
- Incorporating feedback into refined design
- Repeating ... until finished

The extraordinary benefits of collecting and incorporating client feedback into your processes are well understood in many industries. Ken Blanchard, celebrated business effectiveness expert calls feedback, "The Breakfast of Champions." Some designers may be reluctant to systematically utilize client feedback. The biggest reason is often fear.

One fear firm leaders have is that their staff will resist being required to ask for feedback from clients. This is based on an imagined reaction that good staff will be driven from the firm by having to deal with coarse client criticism. Another fear that prevents design firms from utilizing feedback is that the clients themselves will find giving feedback uncomfortable and counterproductive. Both of these fears are based on worst-case scenarios in which the problems are created by a feedback system that is crude and painful.

Since 2000, a group called DesignFacilitator has focused on ways to use technology to boost the prosperity of design firms by utilizing feedback to better communicate with clients. DesignFacilitator integrated their methods into the design industry's first online Client Feedback Tool with customized surveys for architects, engineers, and interior designers. The Client Feedback Tool adds speed and convenience to the entire feedback process, using the following process:

- Collect feedback successfully

- Respond to client feedback

- Refine your firm's processes

- Make benefits sustainable

Successful feedback collection (surveying) involves three key elements: good timing, simple questions, and asking the right people.

Regardless of the project type, the goal is to ascertain whether or not your firm is on the right track from the client's perspective. Even the best firms cannot always stay on the right track, but time spent off track erodes the project's profitability and undermines the design firm's reputation. So, the optimum strategy is to survey often and minimize the time spent off track. A good rule of thumb is to survey after every event (meetings, submittal of design drawings, pricing of project, etc.) or at least once a month for each client during an ongoing project.

Deciding what core issues to question in your client survey should be determined by the event you are surveying. DesignFacilitator distilled the number of core issues to six. This allows a short, simple, but concise survey to be sent to your clients. As a bare minimum, you want to ask about the issues involved in the deliverables you produce (schedule, budget, and accuracy) as well inventory the status of the client-firm relationship (helpfulness, responsiveness, and quality).

It is most constructive to focus on asking about your firm's processes rather than question the personal performance of individuals. It is also wise to make all your questions answerable in a numeric format. This will offer you the ability to view all your client feedback over time and better identify the patterns and trends related to different clients, projects, and skill sets.

Whom to Contact

Determining whom to survey, and who at your firm sends surveys, is related to the culture and goals of your firm. The more focused your firm is on client service, strong relationships, and generating repeat business, the more appropriate it is to have the individuals actually working together on the project (the staff members on your team communicating most directly with their client contacts) sending and receiving surveys. This generates the most benefits for both staff and clients because accountability, recognition, and satisfaction tend to grow for both parties. For firms that focus more on the exclusivity of the product they create and tend to obtain commissions by negotiating with new clients for each project, surveys may be more effective if they flow between the owners or leaders of the client and design firms. In short, surveying will increase the understanding and improve the relationship between the two parties involved.

How you respond to client feedback will depend on your firm, the client, and the nature of the feedback received. If you have made your questions very process-oriented, then your feedback becomes a road map for increasing the value to your client by refining the process of project delivery. Initially, it is important to identify the extreme scores in your clients' feedback. High scores (client was "delighted") can generate healthy praise for the staff who earned that feedback and offer confirmation that the particular process used was very effective. Low scores (client got less than expected) shows your firm (especially team leaders) areas in which staff may have fallen short of expectations and in which the leader's help may be needed to resolve an issue. Long term, this data also gives helpful insight as to what training particular staff may need and for what type of assignments they are best suited. Feedback on your firm's process, as opposed to the individuals on your staff, helps identify and exercise your firm's flexibility in responding to change and adapting to new information. The health of the entire firm is improved when you show clients respect by requesting and incorporating their feedback.

When client communication and understanding are enhanced by the collection of feedback directly from the client, and that feedback is used to fine-tune the design firm's process to increase its value to clients, multiple benefits occur. Clients benefit from a more attentive, better informed, less wasteful design firm. Design firms benefit from more loyal clients, more repeat business, improved staff performance and retention, and fewer problems during projects. Finally, your design staff can benefit from increased awareness and enhanced performance leading to greater personal satisfaction and professional growth.

In short, utilizing a system to collect and incorporate client feedback into your design firm benefits clients and staff and offers the healthiest and most sustainable prosperity for your design firm as a business."

Surveys Help Everyone

As you've seen, this type of survey technique can be very helpful internally as well as to your client. This survey technique allows everyone on your staff to have a much better understanding of what might be happening at any point in any project. Even a slightly negative response from clients can be used as a tool in the ongoing education of you and your staff. This and other management techniques help professional interior designers grow beyond assuming everyone is happy because the bills are paid. As times and challenges change, the adept use of new technology will continue to enhance our abilities to manage clients and their projects in a professional and business-like way. It's also an important improvement in our ability to succeed in a competitive and complex business.

Shipping Around the Corner or Across the Country

Once you have the tools in place, using them properly and efficiently will help you manage your clients. As you adapt the different means of communication to your business' particular style and needs don't forget to make use of some of the more prosaic types of contact. Shipping small parcels containing fabric samples, finish samples, and the like is an important part of your arsenal of communication tools. Depending on the location of a particular client and the type of job, overnight shipping might be the best choice. Although the cost is a little higher, it will accentuate the urgency of the decision you are asking the client to make based on the contents of the package. Including a pre-paid return envelope or pick-up is also a good idea. This type of communication might be less flashy than other types, but it's still very effective in the right situation.

Locally you might even consider a courier service to deliver items that might require a prompt decision. Including an explanation of what is expected from the client when the package arrives is a must. In some instances, all the client will need to do is inspect the items sent and prepare to make a decision at the next meeting. At other times, action of some sort will be required, and clear and concise instructions along with a letter or note of explanation will have to be included. In this instance the delivery service might have to wait for an answer and return it to your office immediately. Establishing a good working relationship with a local delivery or courier service will enhance your ability to react quickly and professionally to any type of communication need. Your client will be impressed with the use of a more personal delivery service and you will have the extra benefit of fast turnaround for any information request you make. Your ability to use each of the available communication tools in the most appropriate manner will set you apart from your peers and raise your management skills both in the eyes of your staff and your client.

How to Use Your Communication Tools

No tool works alone, and your ability to utilize communication tools will be an important facet of your success. Many of these tools might take a little time to master, but as you become more adept at selecting the right type of communication media for a specific task you will find the task becomes easier. And, as your message style becomes more consistent, your clients will become more confident in your abilities to efficiently move their project forward to completion.

Are you beginning to see how the various segments of client and project management meld together to form a successful whole? There are certainly times when I feel as if I'm juggling a dozen balls in the air and no one seems to notice. Your complete understanding of the various working parts of management will help you appear cool, calm, and collected, even when you are in the eye of the storm of client management.

CHAPTER SEVEN
PREPARING THE PRESENTATION

" If you want to make an apple pie from scratch,
you must first create the universe. "

— Carl Sagan (1934–1996)

With a signed contract in hand and a realistic budget with which to work, it is time to put together a presentation for your client. The discussions with the client leading up to the contract have prepared you for what is to come. The likes and dislikes of your client will be an integral part of your decision-making process while creating an interior that will please the client. This is one of the most exciting parts of any project and is ultimately the expression of your talent and abilities as an interior designer. It is also one of the most difficult challenges we face as professionals. The creation of beautiful interiors is certainly what brought most of us to the profession in the first place, and this is the part that is meant to be fun for us. It's fun, but it's also hard work. Once again, organization is the name of this game. Think about chess as an example. There are simple moves, like moving your pawn two spaces forward, and there are more complicated moves, such as moving your bishop four spaces diagonally. Each move impacts what will come after, and thinking ahead is essential. The same applies to the creation and management of a client presentation. If, as I suggest, you create more than one design scheme, the multitude of decisions and counter-decisions could overwhelm lesser mortals. Not you, of course—you're a professional. I wouldn't begin to try to tell you how to put a design scheme together, but the pieces need to be organized into a coherent whole before you even think about bringing the client into your studio. This segment of client and project management requires discipline and an uncluttered mind. Now is not the time to daydream about that trip to Aruba.

Where to Begin?

The biggest question, of course, is where to begin. A good way to start is to take some time to simply sit and ponder the plethora of choices that need to be made over the next few days before putting together design schemes. This is the time when you should consider style, color, furnishings, and how they each relate to the client and the project's needs. Plot your presentation strategy by creating your space plan to reflect those items you believe will be needed in the room or rooms you are designing. Whether your assistant creates the space plan or you outsource the work, you should have a clear idea of what is needed. I won't try to tell you how space planning is done, but suffice it to say an appropriate amount of furnishings and fixtures are needed to create a warm and inviting space. Space planning also helps you make selections based on your budget and design style. In other words, it's the beginning of your shopping list. Once you are satisfied with the space plan, you will be able to turn your attentions to specific pieces, fabrics, trims, and other items needed to create today's modern and luxurious interiors.

Consider the types of furnishings that will be required, whether or not drapery will be needed, and how you will create the flow of fabrics, patterns, and finishes within the space. Try to create three or four separate design ideas for the presentations that will follow. Each of these schemes will have different details but will have some similarities, because you are designing for the same space. These multiple schemes also give you the chance to evaluate items you might not have thought of when you first began to make decisions. I'm not suggesting you spend hours more than necessary, but it is a good idea to stretch your imagination a bit to see where it takes you. You will also be looking for ways to get the clients involved and will need to answer honestly questions about what they will see.

Adding one scheme you know isn't right for the client or the space is a tool many designers use to force the client into saying no to the designer at some point in the presentation. This scheme is often referred to as the "hairy armpit" and is intended to expand the conversation during the presentation to include some negative comments about the design selections. This particular set of selections doesn't need to be so obviously out of bounds as to make everyone laugh, but it should be just far enough off-base that the client finds it easy to negate. For many clients and designers, this opens up the process for more honest and forthright discussions once the client understands saying no won't derail the process or hurt the designer's feelings.

Commercial

Commercial interior design is, by its very nature and requirements, different from residential. The parameters set by the designer incorporate different needs and perspectives. Professional space-planning targets the interior aesthetics, the efficiency of the functional layout, and compliance with local building codes. The final plan will show the best use within the least square footage, thereby resulting in better productivity, higher employee satisfaction, and yearly operating cost savings. For most corporate clients these are the criteria that drive their decisions. Smart-looking and functional are the words that often describe what a commercial client is looking for in design services. Presentation preparation for this type of client probably will not include the "hairy armpit" approach. Mounting selections on boards is often the desired format for reviewing different schemes and design ideas. In some instances there will be only one design scheme to be reviewed. Requests for proposal (RFPs) for commercial design often have such minute details regarding color, style, fabric. and finish that there might be only one very good possibility. Your task in this instance is to create an interior and manage the client in a way that meets the criteria exactly and uses your best ability to select durable and attractive finishes. Expanding beyond the RFP is often difficult if not impossible.

Measurements are important for this type of work, so this project might begin by using a computer-driven system called LaserTech. The word "laser" stands for "light amplification by stimulated emission of radiation." Laser Technology (LaserTech) products calculate distance by measuring the time of flight of very short pulses of infrared light. Any solid object will reflect back a certain percentage of the emitted light energy. This is a highly accurate measurement device. For commercial projects, it is invaluable for creating precise design schemes and floor plans. Once the measurements have been transferred to the CAD computer, the designer knows the measurements will be consistent throughout the project and design phase.

The next step for the commercial designer is the space-planning phase. This initial rough plan will show basic layout, flow, and adjacencies. It may or may not include doors, windows, and 2-D millwork locations. This initial plan will include office, common area, and cubicle block placement. The occupancy calculation, based on the initial plan, will determine existing needs per code within the applicable jurisdiction. Many professional interior designers find this type of resource work exciting and fun. For some, the attention to minute details is attractive. Municipalities create and manage building codes to protect their citizens and these codes require strict adherence to the law. Most commercial interior designers' libraries will contain the latest copy of local jurisdiction codes and requirements for building and occupancy.

How to Shop

No one can tell you exactly how to create the space because that is the unique touch individual designers bring to their projects. What you will be doing, however, is creating, in essence, a shopping list of requirements for the space. Once you've settled on an outline of what you believe you will need for the project, a review of your design library is in order. Assess what you have in terms of furniture, lighting, accessory, and flooring catalogues as well as the depth of your fabric selection. Now consider your library in the context of how it will help you create the space for your client. A large and comprehensive design library within your office space is the optimum choice. Do you have fabrics that are compatible to the style of room and do you feel they are right for your client? Do your furniture catalogues have a large enough selection to give you a wealth of choices, and will you be able to offer enough flooring choices to satisfy the designs? The larger your library, the better the chance you have of finding exactly what you need without taking time from your busy schedule to travel to a design center. Should your library not have enough choices, a trip to the showroom might be in order. Before shopping you should have a list of what you believe you will need, but be sure to add to selections as you see things that inspire you.

When you arrive at the showrooms present yourself to the manager or receptionist and sign in, if required. If you need help locating a specific item, ask for assistance. Most showrooms have staff ready to help you with your selections, and some are qualified interior designers themselves. Don't hesitate to use the resources the showroom offers. You might even be comfortable enough with the design knowledge of some of the staff you meet to telephone them and ask that they make selections to send to your office based on your design criteria. This type of outsourcing could save you hours of time walking the showroom floors and give you another creative eye within the design center. For designers more than two hours away from a big-city showroom, this is an invaluable money saver in the way of hourly time charges to your client. It will also save wear and tear on you and your automobile.

Presentation preparation and selection is demanding work, and you will be focused on the needs of each proposed design scheme. Now is not the time to have the client tag along if you choose to visit the local showrooms. A professional interior designer's job is to pre-select items to be included in presentations. It is not appropriate for the client to come along to help select those items you believe best suit your proposed presentation schemes. It is also time consuming and costly for the client. Most clients will be overwhelmed with the choices available and have no concept of how to reduce the selections to a workable number. That is your job. From a client management point of view, you have a much better idea of what types of finishes, styles, and textures are needed for a particular design scheme. Your clients aren't as adept as you and will slow the whole process down with irrelevant choices or styles. They can become easily distracted and forget exactly why they came along. Honestly, do you really need the company? Although a client's input is important both at the initial interview and final presentation, working together in the showroom is a lazy way to proceed. Use your time and your client's money wisely by working on your own and selecting for the presentation those items and extra selections you feel are appropriate for each design scheme.

Presentation Strategies

Once you've returned to your studio, the organization process begins. There are numerous ways to create a presentation and designers use the things they find comfortable, pleasant, and easy for the client to understand. For many design firms the use of presentation boards is "de rigueur." Their preparation is a job performed by many junior designers across the country. Small swatches, photos, and floor plans are assembled on a large art board that has a background color that will blend in with the scheme. Each design scheme has its own board. For larger projects there will also be separate boards for lighting design and perspective drawings. Although elegant and impressive, creating a presentation board is time consuming and costly for the client unless explained during the contract phase of the project. As interior design students we all created presentation boards as part of larger assignments within the design syllabus, and many designers find boards familiar and easy to work with. There are, of course, other options for presentations.

Many other design firms employ the use of larger fabric samples, full photos, and full floor plans for presentations. For this type of presentation, each segment, whether it's fabric, a floor plan, a photo, or a furniture suggestion, is placed on a large work surface as the designer explains how it will be used within the space. As the presentation moves forward, each piece is revealed within the context of what came before. The room literally unfolds before their eyes, which many clients find exciting and dramatic. For many, simply being able to actually handle the pieces to be included is stimulating and helps them conceptualize the room. Larger samples of all the fabrics, wall coverings, paints, and finishes shown will enhance the presentation and create an arrangement of pieces easy for the client to see and for you to explain. Paint samples from most of the larger firms are available in 3" × 5" sizes as well as 8" × 10" sizes. Some firms I know buy the proposed paint color and apply it to a large piece for presentation. Wallpaper samples are also available in larger formats. The optimum size includes at least one pattern repeat to allow the client to see how the pattern flow will work within the space. From time to time I have ordered a length of hardwood flooring to show how the pattern and finish, particularly for distressed or more exotic pieces, will look within the context of the proposed design scheme.

During the preparation you may decide the need for expanded floor plans, reflected ceiling plans, elevations, or renderings. Each of these is another time consuming aspect of the design process and can be very costly to the designer and the client. If your design firm doesn't have the staff or equipment to prepare these elements, you might consider outsourcing.

The Wonderful World of Outsourcing

Outsourcing is simply the delegation of a business process to an external service provider. Most interior design firms have accountants, attorneys, and Web site designers to whom they have outsourced a service. Outsourcing is not simply a cost-cutting measure, either. By judiciously outsourcing tasks to reputable firms, you will free up time in your office for more profitable endeavors. From a client management standpoint, the economics of outsourcing help keep expenses down for your firm and for your client. There is a huge selection of possibilities for firms to which you can outsource. Although some of the outsourcing firms are not in this country, the vast majority of those you will choose are all within the boundaries of our shores. These companies and services from which you might want assistance will help you control your expenses and will be a resource for your firm only when needed. You are no longer required to hire, with all of the attendant expenses, a full- or part-time employee to perform a particular function within the firm. And, at the same time, you are able to say in all honesty that your firm is capable of any type of CAD, 3-D, or rendering presentation required for any particular project. You will not be giving control of the project away to someone else and in many instances the outsourcing firm may help you refine the concepts you already have in place. You will see more about the benefits of outsourcing other tasks and responsibilities in chapter 10.

A quick perusal of Google reveals numerous companies willing to take your plans and turn them into reality. Most clients will be astounded by the richness of detail and quality of presentation from your outsourcing options. The time it takes to finish your project is often far less than if you produced the same rendering in-house, and the expense is minimal compared to other options. The price varies according to what is needed, but many 3-D renderings start as low as $300 per drawing. How valuable is your time and what could be outsourced? Depending on how much you charge per hour for design time, this could become profitable for your business and enhance the quality and professionalism of your presentations. You might also find the ease with which floor plans, revealed ceilings, and finish schedules are produced will entice you to send more of this type of preparation work to outsourcing firms across the country.

One professional designer I know in Palm Springs, California, sends every detail of most of her presentations to a firm with whom she has worked for three years. She is a sole proprietor with a part-time office assistant/receptionist and no other part-time or full-time staff.

By working closely with the firm from the beginning, she has created a professional rapport she believes enhances her ability to produce renderings and interiors. She has also found it costs no more for her client than if she had a staff on board doing all the tasks she sends out for completion. Turnaround for the detailed and accurate drawings is quick and many can be downloaded to her computer for printing. Overnight delivery is also available and helps the project to move forward in a timely manner. As you will see in chapter 10 many, many other tasks are prime candidates for outsourcing and could bring savings to your firm. As more design firms employ this type of client and project management, your clients will begin to expect it when you present.

How to Put It All Together

As you assemble the various parts of your presentation schemes you should also be thinking about how each scheme should be presented. Your clients will be very interested in how the presentations will unfold, so now is the time to envision how you want to proceed. Creating a powerful and persuasive presentation isn't a matter of chance. Putting together an arrangement of samples, floor plans, renderings, and tear sheets to tell a story and show how beautiful the space can be takes time and patience. You should separate the various schemes you have devised and decide which will come first, second, third, and last. Organization is of utmost importance at this point. Within each scheme many designers start with the space plan and describe how each piece selected works within the confines of the whole. If the presentation includes more than one space, start with the logical opening. You're telling a story here, remember?

If the project is a complete renovation of the home, start with the entryway. Move into the living room, dining room, great room, kitchen, and any other more public spaces to be designed. Do not try to include fabrics, finishes, and accessories at this point. Keeping an organized and logical approach is very good client management and will help keep them focused on the presentation at hand. Move on to the bedrooms, baths, and offices. Once you're finished describing the space planning, you can move on to a room-by-room description of the furnishing, fabrics, and finishes. The day before your clients arrive for the presentation appointment, review all the schemes you will show them. Go one step further and actually run through each presentation as if the client was sitting across the table from you. It will help you discover any missing items from the presentation and will also help you become more comfortable with the items you will be showing. As you become familiar with the specific pieces of each presentation, extolling the virtues of each will be easier.

Take Advantage of Advanced Technology

One of the most advanced types of presentations you might consider is using your computer to literally walk your client through the space. Using various software programs, you can create a virtual reality of the proposed space. As with the previous example, you could start by actually walking through the front door. All furniture and fixtures would, at this point, have no specific colors or patterns—your emphasis is on space planning. Show how the client will be able to walk through the space and how the design will flow through different areas. Once space planning is addressed you can return to the front door, make an adjustment to the presentation style on the software, and add colors and patterns. In many instances you will be able to place exact patterns of fabrics and specific textures of wall coverings within the software program. This is also another task you might want to outsource. You can have the presentation sent to your office a few days before you see the client.

Once you've pulled together a few design schemes, proposal estimates need to be prepared.

You may not want to type up a whole collection of proposals, but handwritten estimates could be in order. Some firms use pre-printed forms in estimating. The designer is able to figure out the pricing of products and services to be offered and integrate those dollars into the overall budget for the client. This process will also help the designer get a good feel for where the budget is going or has gone. If the pricing is way over the agreed-upon budget, the designer has a chance to reselect before the client even comes through the door. This proposal, or worksheet, process also helps to organize the presentation. Having as much written down as possible keeps the design on track and on budget. You may also decide to make each of the prepared presentations have a different price range. As discussed in the previous chapter, many design firms actually offer a range of pricing to allow clients to select what will be most comfortable for them and the project.

Leslie Hassler is the president of Designs by Leslie, Inc., a luxury residential design and decoration firm in Houston, Texas. I've asked Leslie to give us some insight into her firm's presentation preparation style and how it benefits her clientele.

"Preparing for the presentation begins the minute we begin work on a project. As a project manager our job is to supply as much documentation as possible to achieve the best outcome of any presentation. We follow a meeting management principle. We decide what the objective of the presentation will be. Would we like to complete a programming and needs analysis? Are we looking for approval on a general design direction, or are we looking to get specific approval on technical drawings? Once the meeting objective is decided we ascertain what information should be provided to the client in order for all of us to achieve the stated objectives. We also decide what pricing, technical documents, and/or finish samples are needed. The more complete the presentation the better the outcome will be. We discuss with our clients what it is that we hope to achieve in the meeting and what materials we plan on presenting. We then ask if this meets their expectations and if there is anything else we need to address during the meeting. By defining these parameters we will also be able to accurately judge the time it will take to cover the materials with them and arrive at unhurried and thoughtful decisions.

Use Your Library Card

We also decide during the preparation phase how adequate our design library is for the presentation we are preparing. We believe we are a bit more technologically advanced than some interior design firms. Although we have a modest design library, it is more reference/ideation based than catalogue based. The catalogues we do have are often from lines that have a very limited Internet presence or no local showroom presence. Other catalogues are for lines we utilize often and for which we find flipping through the printed material far easier than online searching. Although the design center is a good 30- to 45-minute drive from our office, we still go and look in the showrooms. The Internet is good for narrowing down lines or accessing a line that is not represented in your area, but, as all designers know, one can't select final finishes and samples from it. If time is of the essence, we may use the Internet to pre-select fabrics, but we always have memo samples sent to us to review with all the other materials. Visiting the showrooms also allows us a chance to review new product introductions and possible changes in colors or finishes. Print materials and even the Internet are not always updated with new products. Be aware of what is current and what might fit your project when planning the presentation.

Preparation and the Budget

We start off with a planning budget, which is created shortly after the scope of the project has been defined. Many clients are unaware of what type of investment a project might require and a planning budget begins the process of aligning everyone's expectations. It also enables us to show clients where we suggest placing financial emphasis and allows an opportunity for the client to express where they feel there should be an emphasis. When we present the design concept, we update these budget numbers, but they still aren't the final estimate. Once the design concept is decided upon we complete the estimates. Included in the estimate is everything we can possibly think of, from possible price increases to freight. Shipping, in particular, can be a big surprise to clients. Why not include it in the beginning, so there are no surprises? Let's face it, every client has a budget. Every client wants to stay within his or her budget, and it is your responsibility to ethically manage it.

The elements of the presentation will vary project to project. Whether we are splitting up rooms or phases of construction, we always present it soup to nuts. Not that we can't offer options, but each element needs to be present. If we are designing the kitchen, as part of final presentation we present everything: flooring, lighting, plumbing, appliances, space plan with basic dimensions, cabinetry elevations, finish selections, hardware—the works. Hopefully we've had mini approvals along the way and nothing in the presentation is a complete surprise.

More often, mini approvals were not made for fabric and drapery. For our presentation of window treatments, we check price and stock on everything. We would hate for our client to fall in love with a pattern only to find out that it has been discontinued. We don't want to create disappointment; we want to create excitement. We also price all fabric with client costs per yard and note anything with limited stock yardage. This way, when our clients choose fabric, they are making a decision based on aesthetic and cost. If they love the $100 per yard fabric, they know from the beginning that it costs $100 per yard. We believe if our client isn't aware of the price choices along the way, he or she will feel cheated or lied to. We also present sketches or photographs of the drapery style along with hardware and trim selections. At this point, it is too preliminary to have labor costs in hand, but we should have a basic understanding of the yardages needed.

Samples and Boards

We have only done one presentation board and that was for a commercial loft spec project. Our firm tends to create folders or binders that outline all the selections, finishes, drawings, and fabrics. We like to use as large a sample as possible and include in our presentations 8"-square paint samples, fabric memos, large wall covering samples, and real finish samples the client will be able to touch and feel. If the repeat of a fabric is large, or the sample doesn't do it justice, we will arrange with the showroom to borrow the wing sample. Our presentations generally have the feel of working sessions rather than board presentations. We produce that type of presentation more for commercial work.

Most clients only want to pay for what they feel is absolutely necessary and we have never completed full-scale renderings. We prepare sketches as necessary to convey the design. One reason we have focused on learning 3-D software is to more accurately present our design concept in a manner that all clients can understand. We will never be able to get away from needing AutoCad for technical details, custom designs, and architectural details, but clients understand 3-D so much better. For design projects, the 3-D technique takes about the same amount of time to execute as sketches, forces us to think through more of the project, and allows us to become more efficient and prevent possible problems. When working with our external team of lighting, cabinetry, or case goods designers, we find many of these professionals complete design drawings as part of their services to us and the project. When they are able to provide us with perspectives or elevations, we are able to communicate and sell the job in a more complete manner. It is a value-added service to your client.

Getting All Your Ducks in a Row

Document, document, document and in case you are in doubt, document. As time elapses and you begin to manage multiple clients, you cannot rely on memory alone. You need a detailed contract and an even more detailed scope of the project. Initial proposals may not have every detail documented, but you need to be clear about what is included and what is not included. Your clients will often assume something is included and it is your job to communicate with them what constitutes a complete proposal. We keep journals that are hardbound, not flimsy spirals, and are durable. We try to document everything in these journals and note the client/project and date with each entry. If I have a preliminary conversation with the workroom, my notes are in the journal. Once a purchase order is issued, we put the notes on the purchase order. That way anyone on my team is able to look at the paperwork and know what has been discussed. We keep all of our old journals on our shelves and refer to them to validate details. You never know when you may need it. It is better to have written records than not.

Finally, both in estimating and evaluating the profitability of completed projects, experience will be your best ally. Keep ballpark quotes to a minimum and never give firm quotes until you have researched the items involved. I once worked with a designer who quoted, often incorrectly, prices for items or projects on the spot. Once the project was developed, it became clear the piece was not available or only available at a greater price. Many times she had to honor the lower price because clients were irate to find it would cost so much more than they had been originally told. Never be afraid to say you will need to define more of the details before giving an accurate cost estimate."

Practice Makes Perfect

The accumulation of all the various specifications, samples, and pricing of a presentation prepares you for the meeting with your client. Success depends on your ability to organize efficiently and manage all aspects of what you are about to show. Don't be afraid to spend some time rehearsing the presentation. Go through each scheme as if the client was in the room with you. By reviewing your selections you will also ensure you haven't forgotten anything. The presentation should be seamless, and you want all the design schemes to contain every item you planned on from the beginning.

Practice will give you the security to move forward with a firm understanding of what you hope to accomplish during the upcoming meeting and how best to proceed. With this security will come the ability to actually enjoy what you are about to present to your client. You should have fun. A lot of the creative hard work we do as interior designers is in preparation for presentations. You've accomplished a lot with this preparation. Presentation to the client is not a war and it won't be a battle. It is a time for you to shine as a creative and accomplished professional. It allows you to stretch your wings and bring your clients along for the ride of their lives. You job is to help many of your clients realize a lifelong dream of beautiful surroundings created by a talented interior designer. How could life get any better?

CHAPTER EIGHT

PRESENTING TO THE CLIENT

❝A lot of times, people don't know what they
want until you show it to them.❞
— Apple Inc. CEO Steve Jobs, *BusinessWeek*, May 25, 1998

A s with public speaking, there are interior designers who find presentations somewhat daunting. They needn't be. You created what
you will be showing, so you should have a complete understanding of
the choices you made and why you made them. Your knowledge of the
pieces to be shown is extensive and your ability to explain the benefits of
each comes from the work you did while researching. You have become
so involved with the presentation and its nuances of style, color, and
finish that you are far more prepared than you might believe. Don't be
afraid of the upcoming meeting. This is your time to shine. Your expertise
is unquestionable, and you have the tools to explain any selections you
might have made. At the same time, you should also have the ability to
answer any questions your clients might pose. You're ready, so saddle up
and hit the presentation trail.

Out of Town Audition

For many interior designers the first presentation is like a Broadway
opening. Everything must be fine-tuned for the most effective impact.
You should have held a rehearsal the day before, and, like many rehears-
als, it might have been a little rough around the edges. That's why you
rehearse—to tighten up your thoughts and presentation style before you
go onstage on opening night. Preparation is essential to the successful

display of your design accomplishments and the ultimate satisfaction of your client. As a professional interior designer, you should know how you arrived at the particular choices you made and be able to explain to the client why they are the best selections. The presentation is the time to "strut your stuff" and show the client how the space will come together in a way that will please the eye and satisfy the budget. It is your time to take center stage with the client as your audience. You want to make your presentations exciting and interesting while not overwhelming your clients or impeding their ability to understand and absorb what is presented. As you will see, there are many aspects of the client presentation that will affect the outcome of this particular meeting.

Even before you start working within your office to ensure you have the proper space to present your design schemes, you should consider whether or not you possess all the tools necessary for a successful sale when the curtain closes on your presentation. We'll actually talk about sales in the next chapter but now is the time to consider whether you are knowledgeable enough to present to clients in an interesting and compelling way. One of the best tools I've found to improve my ability to make good presentations is to attend seminars and conferences both in my area and around the country. I am not suggesting you spend all your time on the road but I do advocate at least two national conferences a year and five to seven local seminars or meetings. These types of gatherings not only allow you to meet with and talk to designers from other parts of the country, they are also immensely informative and educational. Generally within the agenda of any national conference, there will be break-out groups designed specifically for those interested in improving their presentation or sales skills. As always there will also be talks on marketing, budget, pricing, and project management. All of this is part and parcel of client management. The important thing to remember about national conferences is the freedom they give you to talk honestly and openly about how you run your business and what, if anything, your peers might suggest you change.

The Safety of Another Neighborhood

Since you are not usually dealing with members of your own design community you can be candid about pricing within your firm, how you handle client questions, and whether or not you feel you're making enough money—things you would probably not share with local designers. National conferences also give you the opportunity to learn how other professional designers operate their businesses. You will be able to improve your presentation and business skills with what you are able to glean from round-table discussions. It's also important for you to define who, among the attendees, you most want to meet. No matter how lofty their business seems or how important you believe they might be, you will be pleasantly surprised to find most designers are willing to talk about the business to other designers. One of the easiest ways for you to meet these people is to simply stand in a group or join a round-table discussion in which they are participating. Don't stalk them and don't interrupt conversations, but introduce yourself and explain how you feel their input will benefit your business and your understanding of how best to approach a specific question. As you meet these other designers you will also want to enjoy meals with them and get to know them on a more casual level. This, too, is important for keeping in touch once the conference is concluded. And be sure to maintain that contact. The privilege and security of having mentors from across the country or, if you're lucky, around the world, is a great addition to your client and project management portfolio. They are always there to help, and that will help you succeed in managing your clients and their projects.

Home Court Advantage

Local seminars are far easier to attend and less costly but don't usually give you the large scope of a national conference. Still, meeting with other local designers will give you a wonderful perspective on what is happening in your design community. It's also important for your clients to know you attend these local gatherings of designers and you are a respected member of that community. These local gatherings will help you improve your ability to meet and talk to other designers. Then, when you go to a national convention, you won't be as unsure of yourself as you might have been. Local seminars are also usually a great place to find out about new craftsmen in the area and who is working with whom on what projects. You need to know how busy everyone is and where the projects are coming from. That kind of local information will help you judge whether or not you are getting your fair share of the business. Remember, however, some people are prone to exaggeration and you will have to take what you hear with a little grain of salt. It's just the way our world works; get used to it.

Once you have a few seminars and national conferences under your belt, you'll be far more adept at creating and presenting an up-to-the-minute, exciting presentation. The knowledge you continue to accumulate will help you be more comfortable talking to clients and believing you have presented the best possible solutions to their design dilemmas.

Staging

One of the first things you will want to do is prepare the space in which the presentation will take place. Many design studios have walls lined with samples and catalogues, with a large, high work table as the center of the space. The table is large enough to display the numerous combinations of schemes you will show and allows easey access for you and your clients. Usually the work table is around thirty-six inches to thirty-nine inches high and somewhere in the range of fifty-four inches to sixty inches wide by about seventy-two to eighty-four inches long, which allows for easy sample placement and visibility. There should be enough seating for the clients as well as you, the designer, that is tall enough for the table. Barstools are wonderful choices, as they help clients feel they are part of your working environment and a part of the decisions. Being perched at eye level with you while you stand also helps to make them feel engaged as you present the schemes you've prepared. The work table, as opposed to a conference table, also engages clients and makes them feel a part of the work that is being done.

Lighting is important. You should have color-balanced fluorescents above the work table and along the walls. Incandescent lamps skew the color balance of fabrics and are often hard to tolerate for long periods of time. Incandescent lamps also throw out a lot more heat and can make the presentation area uncomfortable after a few minutes. There should be an area in which to stage the upcoming presentation packets or boards that is easily accessible for you and doesn't require you to leave the space while presenting. I always make sure I have pads on which to write notes and pens or pencils readily available. Once you are satisfied that everything is ready, spend a moment clearing your mind and adjusting your mood for meeting your clients. There is no need to go into a Zen-like trance, but do allow yourself time to catch your breath and calm your nerves.

. . . And Showtime

When the clients arrive, usher them into your studio presentation area and make them comfortable. Take coats, if not already taken by your receptionist or office manager, and show the clients where you would like them to sit. If you have decided to offer some sort of refreshment, have it available and ready to serve. This allows you and the clients a bit of time for a little small talk before you segue into the presentation. You might speak a little about how much you have enjoyed preparing what they are about to see. Assuming one of your schemes is a little different from what you previously discussed, now would be a great time to give them a little warning by saying something like, "I hope you will be pleased with a couple of things I've decided to show you that might be more of a stretch stylistically," or, "I decided to tweak the design in a direction we haven't discussed, but I believe you will find it fresh and exciting." Don't start throwing out samples at that time. This is just like the overture for a musical. You are warming them up for the first act. This part of the presentation shouldn't last long—you will know when it's time to move on. Once it becomes obvious the small talk has been exhausted, begin the presentation.

The opening phrases of your presentation should be light and can include an explanation of how you will proceed. If you have decided to use large samples and photos, ask the clients to let you present the complete scheme before breaking in with questions. Explain that you expect them to have questions and there will be plenty of time for them once the schemes have been completely revealed. The same applies to boards–you want the chance to explain all the components of each scheme before the questions begin. As you unfold the schemes to the client, be sure to keep talking about each design idea and why you chose the particular pieces you are showing. Babbling is not good, so you need to have worked on your explanations when you rehearsed the day before. Show excitement and real interest as you put the items on the presentation table. If you're not interested and excited, how can you expect the clients to become engaged? Talk about how each piece coordinates with the others and how it is going to flow to create the interior they want.

If you have chosen to show more than one scheme, you might also show how certain components of each could work with another design idea. You could also have a few tricks up your sleeve that might look like sudden thoughts of inspiration. I'm not encouraging you to be evil or deceptive here, but giving the presentation a certain impromptu edge will keep everyone engaged and interested. Clients love to see their designer step away for a moment to grab that "just right" piece of trim or co-ordinate fabric for the scheme that is being presented. It creates a feel of unexpected surprise around every corner and engenders true excitement within your client. Excitement is what opens up your clients' ability to answer honestly what they like and dislike about any particular scheme.

Any Questions?

Once all of the schemes you want to present are on the table, ask your clients for their thoughts and questions. From experience, I know they will ask if any of the fabrics can be changed from one scheme to another. One scheme might be in shades of blue and another in shades of yellow. Since most fabrics come in several different colors, a change can usually be made if the patterns still work with the scheme in question. Your clients will want to know if the sofa fabric will work on the chair and if the rug can be made larger. They will ask about lighting and accessories and whether or not a different cocktail table can be found for scheme number three. Each of these questions and more will be part of the interrogation you will undergo, and it's your job to answer within the context of the presentation and scheme. If some things simply cannot be changed, say so. Other changes might be as simple as finding a slimmer lamp or larger rug. Just be sure you know why you made the selections in the first place. Your preparation before the presentation will be invaluable now.

This part of the presentation should also not be allowed to run over the ninety-minute limit you might have set for the length of the meeting. Even when asking questions, the clients will eventually become tired and possibly overwhelmed by the choices they are now being asked to make. Don't let that happen. Give them a chance to catch their breath by suggesting wrapping up the meeting to allow you time to make any requested changes and to update the budget figures. You will also have the opportunity to flesh out a particular scheme or idea that might have presented itself during the presentation. The art of interior design isn't meant to happen overnight. It shouldn't drag on forever, but a controlled and thoughtful process is in order.

Are We Having Fun, Yet?

I have always enjoyed presentations. Clients generally become very involved and give you a lot of feedback—most of it positive. Now, however, is the time when you want to hear them say no to something you have presented—hopefully the hairy armpit presentation. Why, you ask, do I want to hear my client say no? It's important that clients understand a no from them is not going to run the design train off the tracks. I want them to see that I am in no way upset by their choice to delete one scheme or fabric and am happy to search for a replacement if needed. Once they see that the sky is not going to fall on the presentation table if they choose not to work with one of the schemes presented, the process becomes smoother and easier to manage. It also opens up the discussion for a more honest and forthright dialogue about the process as a whole. From now on clients won't hesitate to tell you exactly what they think of anything you present. You will also find they begin to have a lot more trust in your ideas. They now know you aren't working from ego but a true desire to please them and make the best possible selections for their project.

During this part of the presentation, you will also find out what your clients are really interested in from a design standpoint. Hopefully they will have gravitated to a particular scheme you have presented and are beginning to talk about how it will fit into the new space they have decided to have you create. Now is not the time to try and push them into numerous decisions. Your presentation has already taken up a lot of time, and most clients burn out after about ninety minutes. You might extend some presentations to two hours, but even that is pushing it. My experience has always shown ninety minutes to be the optimum time for a presentation. I promise the decisions made after that time will be reversed or second-guessed. You might have to divide your presentations between two or three meetings to ensure your clients are fully engaged in the process. When their eyes start to glaze over and they aren't asking a lot of questions, you know it is time to bring the meeting to a comfortable close. After this first presentation is a good time for you to take the choices that have been made and refine the whole scheme. Additions can be made to the overall plan and pricing can be refined to show specific selections.

Tag-Team

If you have a support staff, a "tag-team" approach to your presentation might be in order. I'm not talking Saturday night wrestling here. Simply put, a tag-team uses the special skills of each participant to present the design schemes in the best possible way. One of you might begin with small talk when the clients arrive to get them comfortable and ready for the presentation. You might then turn to the second staff member to present the first scheme. Don't show your best ideas with the first scheme, but don't make it the hairy armpit scheme (if you've chosen to have one). Make it your second best attempt, and follow it with what you consider to be the best solution to the design challenge presented by the clients. You might find, when presenting the second scheme, that having you and your tag-team partner both participate will help you to more effectively explain how each part of the scheme works with the others to create a harmonious whole.

Understand that with this type of presentation you and your partner mustn't step on each other's toes. Don't jump in to explain something you feel the other hasn't covered completely. Wait until an opportune moment to add whatever comments you feel are necessary. Also, try to avoid making the clients feel like the two of you are trying to gang up on them. Each of you should listen to the clients and answer any questions they may have, regardless of where you are within the planned presentation. Together the two of you will work through the design scheme and highlight each part with your own particular presentation and selling style. The intent is to make the client feel comfortable with the presentation and with each of the presenters. As you can imagine, tag-team presentations require the same amount of rehearsal as single presentations. Working together to smooth out the rough edges also makes for a more seamless story for the client.

Let's Take This Show on the Road

From time to time, you may feel the need to present to the clients in their home rather than your office. For some projects, this is the only way to show a design scheme to its best advantage. Many interior designers have very small offices, work out of their homes, or find clients who are more comfortable working in their own space. Taking your presentation out of the office adds to the excitement of what you will show and, at the same time, requires you to have with you all the items you have included in your presentation. As with presentations in your office, presentations in clients' homes or other spaces must be fully prepared and put together. You should not arrive with bags and bags of samples and tear-sheets. Restrict the items you bring to only what is needed to convey exactly what the new design schemes will involve.

Marlene Oliphant, of Oliphant Designs, LLC, in Glendale, California, shows her presentations in the client's space as opposed to her office. She finds the clients more responsive to her ideas and believes it makes closing the sale easier when the client is in their own surroundings.

"I have a small home office, do only residential design, and always do my presentations in the client's home. That way it's easier to describe what goes where, since I show them the floor plans, fabrics, and materials, but thus far have not had the budget to do renderings. Sometimes elevations help when they are needed for construction/electrical plans. I usually allow one hour for a presentation or more if multiple rooms are involved. My presentations do not include boards, and I show each element by providing photographs for each piece of furniture and actual fabrics samples. I provide the clients with a notebook in which I insert tear-sheets of the items discussed and color copies of the fabric samples. There is no information on brand names or item numbers, but I do show pricing on each sheet. The clients are able to follow along as I present the design scheme, and the book proves particularly helpful when there is more than one room or space in which we are working. They are able to follow along in the client book and see exactly what each piece will look like in each space.

Enthusiasm Is Infectious

I try to convey a lot of excitement for the project and the items I have found for clients. I want them to know that I have approached their project as though I have no other, that their design is totally unique to them, and that I am very excited for them to see the outcome. I always have at least one, two, or sometimes three "wow" items that are above their budget. Some more affluent clients may not set a budget figure from the beginning and simply want to see what I have to offer. Even they are "wowed" by my special items. I do not show these items first; I work up to them, and I see the clients becoming more excited when I present the most stylish and sometimes most expensive items that will unmistakably complete the entire look. I present them in such a way as to show that if the upscale items are left out, the design simply won't be the same. I have never had a client turn down this type of item for the sake of the budget. Of course I always have alternatives ready to show, including extra fabrics and some additional light fixtures. If, for a bath or kitchen design, they want to see additional choices of tile or stone, I schedule a trip to the store with them to make the final selections.

In my six-year history as a professional interior designer I have not had a problem with couples disagreeing. Usually it's the wife who looks at the presentation. In this instance the husband prefers to see the finished product. We are making all the selections while he is working, and the wife is making all of the decisions. When I see the husband, I always ask him how he feels about how the design is evolving to make him feel included. There is always something in the design specifically tailored to him, so I can ask about it and make sure he sits in the chair, for example, or the sofa to be sure it fits him and he likes it before ordering. One of my client couples has the reverse situation. The husband is doing all the decision-making and the wife goes along. I do make sure she is available when we are making important decisions, as it is the kitchen we are designing, and she will be the one cooking.

It is important, as in any interaction with clients, to observe the nonverbal behavior, and to be quiet sometimes to elicit a response from the client. I always allow clients to express their opinion, suggest they feel the fabrics, and make sure they feel a part of the process. My clients love having their notebooks with all details of the design in them, and they use them to add tear-sheets as I provide them. The use of the client notebook also allows them to feel that the redesign/ remodel is actually happening and that this is a plan that will be carried out and followed through by my office.

Getting the Deposit

At the end of the presentation I have the purchase orders ready for them to sign so I can collect the deposit for the furnishings, fabrics, lighting, and anything else needed to get the project going. For items such as flooring and tile, the subcontractor may not have measured the spaces and provided estimates yet, but I give the client a ballpark figure based on my preliminary measurements and collect those deposits, as well. I explain the subcontractor has the final say on the amounts of material needed and it is possible the final total will change. If possible, I always try to have firm figures for items to be ordered. By the end of the presentation the clients have a relatively accurate budget figure for my portion of the project.

The success of making a good presentation also depends on having done my research with clients beforehand. I try to get to know their needs and desires as much as I can before making choices for them. I want them to know during the presentation that I have truly listened to their wishes and ascertained their needs accurately. I want them to know I care deeply about their welfare and their happiness in the new space. I became a professional interior designer because I like helping people with their personal spaces. It is a privilege to be able to enhance people's lives with good design, and a joy when I hit it right on, especially if I am able to see that the client feels that way, as well."

Be Creative

The presentation is such a crucial part of what you do as a professional interior designer that thinking about other, more innovative ways to present is important. We want our clients to be involved and excited about what they will see and, we hope, purchase. There's nothing wrong with adding a little spice from time to time. Whether you present at your clients' homes or in your own studio, it's a good idea to bring along a couple of surprises. It could be, as in Ms. Oliphant's presentations, an over-the-top item the client never would have thought of without you. You might decide to add a special trim or ribbon to an otherwise bland, Roman-style shade. Mixing up different patterns within the same space makes for exciting rooms with just the slightest amount of tension. Whatever you decide to add, make sure it is sensible and fits with the vision of the space you have designed. I've spoken about the importance of how you present and of being fully prepared. Sometimes all you need is a little ribbon and tissue paper to create just the right sense of drama for your presentation.

Ribbons and Bows

Phyllis Harbinger, ASID, CID, is the principal for Design Concepts/ Interiors, LLC, serving both commercial and residential clients in the New York Metropolitan area since 1993. She's as comfortable working on a suburban residence as she is in a sleek, modern, city apartment. In fact, the combination of commercial and residential projects and the variety of locales and styles in the New York City region fuel her creativity.

"We do not conduct presentations in my studio. Our firm conducts all presentations at clients' homes or offices at times convenient for all participants. We create two schemes for each space and present them in a unique fashion. We designed and created our own Design Concepts/Interiors bags and use these to transport our fabrics and samples to the presentation site. The fabrics for each room or area are tied together in black and white grosgrain ribbon, wrapped in black and white polka dot tissue paper, and placed in the Design Concepts/Interiors bag. The achromatic black and white patterns do not detract or conflict with any color scheme we may have selected for the client and, we believe, enhance the impact of the colors to show. The clients feel as if we are unwrapping a gift for them. This is a unique and special experience for them, tailored specifically for the rooms to be discussed. We also do quick color sketches to indicate how the space will look, which helps to sell our design concept.

A Personal Portfolio

Space plans and furnishings are presented in a black, portfolio-style book by room and/or space. The clients' names are on the title page and we suggest they bring this book with them to each subsequent meeting. Once the client has made decisions on fabrics, paint, finishes, and accessories we add color copies of those items to our book and update the client's copy as well.

We make sure to keep the discussion on the fabrics, furnishings, and finishes and not on the budget. By actually taking the fabrics and finishes with the suggested layouts into the clients' space, they can see just how things will look in their particular light during different parts of the day. We believe this is a strong selling tool, and it works every time!

I really do not have issues when both clients are involved in the decision-making process. Perhaps because I also have a background in psychology, I have found it easy to facilitate a give and take between both parties and act as a mediator to make sure each one gets something he or she is happy with. An interior designer must really listen, watch the body language, and ask questions. Do not assume that the clients understand your pitch or even your concept. Ask them what they like and dislike. Ask what else, if anything, they wish to see in the space. We work with our clients, because it may be our vision we are bringing to life, but the clients are ultimately going to live in the space, and they must love it."

It's Your Party

Once the presentation has concluded, ask again if there are any questions from your clients.

Usher them out of the area in which you conducted the presentation and help them with their coats or any personal items. Walk them to the door of your office and repeat when you will be seeing them again.

Explain that you will organize proposals requiring their signatures and deposit and let them know when they can expect that paperwork. Don't let the goodbyes last forever. Walk them out, finish the conversation, and say goodbye.

The style in which you ultimately choose to present will be defined by your client's needs and what makes you most comfortable. You will find your style may change over time as you continue to attend conferences and seminars around the country. As your breadth of knowledge increases, your ability to adjust each presentation to a specific client will be enhanced. The ease with which you present and the design expertise you bring to each presentation is most important. You should be secure in the choices you've made for your client and your ability to explain those choices in a clear and concise manner.

As you refine the design schemes selected and prepare the proposals, start thinking about the upcoming sale. As you will see, the sale is very important to the success of your business and your ability to continue to practice interior design in your community.

CHAPTER NINE
THE CLIENT AND THE SALE

> " In the modern world of business, it is useless to be a creative original thinker unless you can also sell what you create."

— David M. Ogilvy, "The Father of Advertising"

Many professional interior designers over the years have shied away from the art of the sale for fear of seeming crass and pushy. Some of the monolithic interior design organizations have even gone so far as to declare that selling has nothing whatsoever to do with professional interior design and professional designers shouldn't demean themselves by selling as if they are simple shopkeepers. I'm here to tell you that day has long gone. The art of selling is an important part of interior design, and a good sales technique is important to client and project management. There are numerous ways to sell products and services, and many more to markup the same services and products for profitability. The combination of a smooth, well-conceived sales style with a consistent and realistic markup policy should be part of your overall business plan. Within this is the key to business success. A good sale involves your abilities to persuade your clients of the optimum choices for any given space, and to make them comfortable with what you charge for your skills. It's not an easy task and is one that requires a thoughtful and humble approach.

Profit

The joy of creation is what brought you to interior design, and you have the right to make a living with your chosen profession. Interior design is your way of making your mark in the world and keeping a roof over your head. This requires the ability to generate an income. Creating, elevating your status in the community, and making a fine living are all very lofty ideals to which you should aspire, but let's come down to earth for a minute. They are part of the overall package of your career as a professional interior designer and one can't exist without the other. So the art of sales is about earning a living and running a profitable and respectable business. Profit is not an ugly word—without it, you won't be able to create all those lovely rooms. Without a steady income you won't be able to advertise your services, pay your staff, outsource space planning, or pay yourself. In short, you won't be able to continue as a professional interior designer.

Markup should include all aspects of your business, not just furnishings and fittings. Hourly time should also be part of your overall profit strategy. The intellectual property you share with each and every design scheme you create for your clients is valuable and should make a profit for your firm. Its contribution to your firm's financial success should go beyond simply covering your expenses. There should be an added value you place on hourly fees to ensure you are paid a salary at the end of each month.

The ideal business you imagine, which includes creative freedom, a heightened visibility in the community, and paying everyone's salaries, should also include the challenges you will face as the one to whom everyone turns for direction. You're in control and managing your clients, their projects, and your interior design firm. As President Harry Truman once said, "The buck stops here." Scary, isn't it? Get ready, we're about to ride the roller coaster of the art of the sale, markup, and client management.

Aren't Design Fees Free Money?

For most of you, I would guess one of the first things you sold your clients was your time. Your design fee was included in the letter of agreement or contract, right? So, how did you arrive at that figure? In the beginning, you might have simply charged what everyone else was charging, but that's not the right approach. Your fees should be based on your expertise and experience as a professional. It might be possible for you to charge more than other designers in the area because of your ability to market more effectively or get better press. Your fees will also be affected by your business overhead. Large offices, fancy cars, and an ample staff all contribute to the equation of hourly fee setting.

Let's take a look. No matter what others say, there is an overhead attached to every movement you make, from the moment you step into your office until you turn off the lights in the evening. No matter what task you perform, there should be an overhead charge attached. To get to a sale, you, as a professional interior designer and project manager, need to understand how important costs and profits are to a successful business. This will enhance your client management skills by enabling you to understand what, exactly, you are selling when you present to a client. As you become more comfortable with that idea, you will be able to sell with ease.

Don't Be Afraid to Increase Fees

Design fees are not just free money coming in. After all, you deserve to be paid for your time just as any other designer in your office. By looking at how much you pay yourself, you will have a good idea of what the net cost of your time is. Add something for profit and you will define the cost of an hour of your time to your client. Add the cost of overhead associated with you being in the office to the cost of your salary, and you will begin to see how much your hourly fee should be. If you've been charging $100 for hourly time and it costs your company $77.50 to have you on site, the profit is only $33.50, or a profit margin of only 23 percent. Not a particularly stellar performance. You need to look for ways to increase that profit margin. One of the best ways I've found to increase the margin of profit on hourly fees is to increase the amount you charge for that hour of your time. I actually advocate raising fees at least once a year.

Don't worry, this needn't be a drastic change. In our business an increase of one percent is huge. Now try five percent. Taking your fees from $100 to $105 will increase your profit margin to 26 percent. A three percent increase in margin of profit is great. Although you may think $5 an hour isn't enough to really matter, consider this: If your billable time is in the neighborhood of 45 to 50 percent of the time you spend in your office each week, a three percent increase to your bottom line could amount to over $5,000 a year. What could you do with that money? How do you feel about that paltry three percent now?

If you do that once a year for three years, it will enhance your bottom line for design fees by over 10 percent, and most clients won't even notice. Selling your expertise as a professional interior designer is an important part of your overall business plan and should be included in any conversation you have with your peer group about markup, overhead, and profit. As the principal of your firm, your time is more valuable than that of your staff. Your staff overhead must always be included in any calculation you make for pricing. Remember, they will be working the orders once the sale is completed and you have moved on to the search for new clients and other client presentations.

Markup

Once you have decided on your hourly design fee, your attention should turn to markup on furnishings, fittings, and services. Most professional interior designers realized many years ago that a set markup on products of only 35 percent wasn't enough to cover the overhead of offices, staff, and procurement. This would create a profit margin of only 26 percent. For far too long, some designers have declared they make up the overhead difference with hourly fees. Unless the fees are extortionately large there will still be a shortfall between expenses and income, which is a loss for your business. Once again, there are a number of ways for you to enhance your bottom line when it comes to the sale of furnishings, fittings, and services.

Raising your markup percentage is one way, and most design firms across the country have done just that. If you insist upon clinging to the old way of having an add-on markup you could, of course, simply increase your add-on fee by a few percentage points. That isn't really addressing the fundamental problem, however, of how best to increase revenue.

A Precious Bundle

One of the best ways is to start to package your products in a way that is easy for the client to understand and, at the same time, gives you more control over the overall markup. Rather than pricing the draperies as individual pieces of fabric, hardware, lining, and installation, bundle the totals into a single dollar amount, add the markup you have defined as necessary to maintain your office, and present this number to the client as a total price. At this time, I usually add trim, interlining, or some other add-on to increase the value of the product and enhance the design. Generally, clients love this part of the sale and are aware of the value in the added component. I know some of you are going to argue that I just set a retail price. You're right, I did. When you simply add a percentage to the price you charge your client you, too, are setting a retail price. Anyone who sells a product above the price it cost them is selling retail. Now that we've clarified what retail means, let's look again at how important the markup is to the overall health of your business and your ability to manage your clients.

The art of the sale, of course, is not just about products and furnishings. You sell your services, too, whether it's design time, drawings, or project management. This area is a wonderful opportunity to create additional profit. Whether it's the more visible services like drawing or order procurement or the relatively hidden service of a simple delivery, a markup should be attached to every cost associated with those tasks. After all, someone has to see to it that the item gets packed, a freight bill is written, and a pick-up issued to ensure that fabric sample goes to the vendor. You will be paying someone's salary to accomplish those tasks, and having the money from the markup on that service to contribute to that payment is helpful.

Regardless of you how you markup your goods and sell them to your clients, you must make a profit large enough to stay in business. You also need to pay the salary of each individual working in your office, including you. The financial status of your business is a direct result of how well you manage markup, overhead, and client sales. A healthy financial picture for your company will increase your clients' respect for your abilities as a businessperson, making them more inclined to work with you and spend money on the products and services you provide. Don't be afraid to charge for what you provide.

Who's Got The Money?

At this point, I believe many design firms and designers lose sight of what is needed. A designer must remember that the clients are the ones with the money and what we, individually, might consider expensive the client might find very affordable. Many years ago I was working with a nationally famous sports personality and his beautiful wife. I decided to create custom bar stools for an area of the large bar/family room we decided they would use for displaying his many awards and trophies. Once I created the design and style of the chairs, chose ultrasuede as the fabric, and defined twelve as the magic number of chairs, I was amazed to discover each stool would cost just over $2,700 each. I certainly couldn't afford to pay that amount of money for bar stools. Then I remembered I had just read in the paper the figures of his recent contract negotiations for the upcoming season. Even a dozen bar stools would require he work for only three and one half hours to pay for them in full. His relative income compared to other clients and me was the important aspect of the equation. I couldn't afford that price for bar stools, but he certainly could. As a matter of fact, we went on to include two new sofas, eight lounge chairs, four ottomans, and four game table chairs with the order, all in ultrasuede, creating the largest order for that product Stroheim & Romann ever had. Once I stepped back from my own prejudices about price I was able to more easily understand how pricing could help make my interior design firm more profitable and professional. The clients were happy with the look of the new room and because I didn't predicate my choices for them on what I, personally, would have spent, we were all pleased, and my firm continued to prosper.

I continue, to this day, to shop at the most exclusive and high-end shops around the world. It is vital that professional interior designers know what is newest, trendiest, and most fashionable on the world market. By comparing the very best of the best to other options, you will also become a savvy shopper for your client. Understanding good value for money isn't just about finding the most inexpensive item. Good value has to be measured against a similar product with the same finish or look. Cheap is just cheap and junk is still junk, so don't confuse the two. Good value for money is always something we need to continue to define for ourselves and for our clients. Oh, and by the way, when I'm out shopping at all these fancy stores I leave my personal credit card at home. I can't afford all that stuff. This is about what my clients can afford, not me.

The Art of the Sale

A masterful sales technique delivered with ease and authority will appeal to clients and maintain your position as manager of the project. Clients will be more comfortable with the process if you are comfortable presenting pricing and payment methods. How you prepare for the sale is as important as presentation preparation. Through design school and beyond, very little thought, if any, is given to the art of the sale. Most colleges and universities spend no time teaching sales techniques to designers seeking any degree. Even those who aspire to achieve a master's degree in business aren't taught the basics of good salesmanship. It's a shame, because selling is something many of us do without even thinking about it. Spending time learning the basics will bring rewards for your business and will certainly make client management easier for you. You sell your ideas to associates, other business owners, and designers every day of the year. It isn't really all that hard.

Ask and You Shall Receive

As with any work of art, the beginning is important. Having a firm grasp of what you already know and understand will help you create your personal sales technique. We are, in essence, talking about how you can get what you want. A sale is getting what you want for the product or service you are showing to your client. It isn't ego-centric to believe in yourself, your product, or your service, and this shouldn't appear crass or crude to you or your client.

From an early age, each of us learned how to ask for what we needed or wanted. At first we simply cried our heads off and got what was needed. We then moved on to temper tantrums and kicking the floor. We finally began to see that these attempts were flawed and slowly adjusted the way in which we asked for something. We learned that a small amount of flattery or a compliment, no matter how transparent, worked wonderfully well on adults. As we grew into our teens, we added a more subtle approach and incorporated more suggestive phrasing. We also learned as teenagers the importance of being responsible for our own needs and to work towards resolving our perceived want. The ability to take responsibility for fulfilling our own wants also helped us understand how valuable owning something could be. As adults in the working world, we have learned to be direct without being demanding. We have incorporated all we learned from childhood into requesting the things we want. All of this is the essence of the art of the sale. Where to begin? As you will see, a good sales technique is an organized and beautiful combination of want and need.

A good sales technique, like a beautiful piece of music, has a beginning, a middle, and an end. The difficult part is learning how to read the score and play the music. Generally speaking, a sales presentation has a gentle beginning, which then moves to a more exciting level of exposition and continues to a rapid exchange of themes. During the exchange part of the sale, questions are answered and thoughts about the purchase are shared. As the sale draws to a close, the interaction slowly relaxes until completion. Understanding how to control each level is the heart and soul of a good selling technique. If the music metaphor doesn't work for you, think about a good book. In the first chapter you are introduced to the characters, the locale, and the plot. Once you understand all the players, the book moves on to an interaction between the characters and some sort of tension, or stress, that moves the story forward. There may be a car chase, an explosion, or a thunderstorm. All are part of moving the drama of the story forward and keeping the reader interested in what is to come. The end brings a resolution of the tensions, ideas, and plot and satisfies readers' desire to see everyone live happily ever after. A professional sales technique resulting in a sale usually leaves everyone feeling happy and satisfied. Each of these examples explains how selling is so much more than simply telling the client the price of something.

Beyond Words

You must be aware of your clients' every move, eye signal, and gesture. With those telling signs you will understand where your clients are in terms of comprehending what you are saying, and you can predict how they will respond. Many times the clues to your clients' responses to your sales technique are subtle and hard to define. Watching them as you produce fabric swatches, finishes, accessory suggestions, or furniture pieces and listening to what they say or, even more importantly, what they don't say will help you know where you are in the process of the sale. Small talk and expressions of pleasure are certainly good signs and will help you move forward to the next level of the sale. Making direct eye contact with clients is important in understanding how they are receiving what you are saying. If clients fold their arms across their chests, turns slightly away from you, or won't make eye contact, you should backtrack a little to engage them again. Ask your staff to hold all calls during this process, and ask your clients to turn off their cell phones. Breaks in concentration will stall the sale faster than anything you might or might not say. A quiet and calm environment is best when trying to make sales comfortable and interactive for your clients.

The words you use are important and a command of language will serve you well. You needn't have a degree in English literature but use words in a way that show your ability to explain clearly and distinctly what you are presenting. Many designers I know have employed the services of a voice or acting coach to help expand their ability to speak to clients in a positive and controlled way. As with the presentation, prepare how you will approach the sale and what will be said to encourage the client to sign on the dotted line.

In the Beginning

The way you begin the sale is important. Don't jump in by telling clients what they need or don't need. Take a subtle approach to help everyone relax and feel involved. Pretend you are around a campfire and are about to tell a really good ghost story. You don't begin by setting a grisly scene with a loud voice; you bring everyone closer to the fire by speaking in a low and controlled voice and setting a calm scene. Start the sale with a gentle approach and slowly explain how each new part of the whole will work with the others. This is the exposition of your sale, and a broad overview of what is to come is part of the technique. Explain how you will be showing each piece of the whole presentation in a sequence intended to unfold plans for the new room like a beautiful flower. Yes, the sale is part of your presentation. Having these two parts work together smoothly is the key to success. As you begin to generate excitement, the level of interaction will increase.

Allow your client to ask questions but don't get derailed by items that might not be directly related to the presentation and sale. Setting the rhythm and tone is very important, and stopping in the middle of your first fabric swatch to talk about the budget isn't going to help move the sale forward. If, during any part of the preliminary and secondary portion of the sale, the client becomes distracted by topics not related to the sale, you might want to discontinue the presentation and set a time for another meeting in the future. Discussions about budget, lighting, and contractor problems at an inopportune time can stop a sale in its tracks. Be very aware of what is being discussed and how it affects your ability to control the conversation.

As you move to the middle of the pitch, you will increase the pace and use words with a little more punch. Occasionally refer back to a previous item or furniture piece to enhance the explanation of what is on the table. I find that a short review at least once and possibly twice during the presentation and sale is instrumental in helping clients understand and remember what they are seeing. Generally, most questions will be asked during the middle phase of the presentation and sale, and you must take the time to answer questions and keep your clients focused. Your clients will probably ask how fabrics or colors relate, how finishes on furniture should match, and whether the drapery should have trim. All of these details are important and are things you can address with ease and aplomb. After all, you are prepared for this and have already thought about many of the things the client is asking about.

As you approach the close of the sale, you don't want to shout at your clients, and you want to make sure they are still interested and engaged in what you are showing. By the time you reach the end of your prepared presentation, you will be ready for even more questions, and the clients will have a few. Give complete and distinct answers. Questions and answers are, after all, the give and take of a good sales technique. As you wrap up, allow clients to absorb what has been said and let them ponder the whole presentation.

Body Language

Your body language as you try to make a sale is a key component of a superior sales technique. As with the presentation, you don't want to be dressed in a way that will distract your clients. As you begin the sale, put samples out for the clients to study, but do not intrude yourself into the scheme. Stay slightly removed from the work table, put samples, photos, or finishes out quickly, and move back from the table to allow the client to see each piece as it's presented. As you progress to the central part of your sale and the table is rich with layers of color and fabric, you can become more engaged and offer a warmer approach to presentation. Hand samples to your clients and ask them to feel the beautiful mohair you have suggested for the sofa. Show them the intricate screening content of a printed fabric and explain what eight-way, hand-tied upholstery means. In short, make them a part of the production. On occasion, I step over to the clients' side of the work table and look at the presentation from their perspective. I don't touch the clients, but continue my conversation about what I am showing with them at my side. I don't stay long and I go back to the other side of the table to show even more items for the design scheme.

The Closing

As you bring the sale to a close pull back just a little but make sure the clients know you are very interested in what they have to say about what you just presented. Although this may not be a symphony or a ghost story, it certainly will be music to your ears when they ask about how to proceed. This is when you literally *make* the sale. In truth, it's your clients who will ask for the sale. They will say something like, "OK, how do we proceed?"

or, "When can we get all this installed?" Whatever they say, you will know you have succeeded. After the work of preparing the presentation and sale, you might find this a little anticlimactic. It isn't. Simply put, you present your pricing and explain what deposit is needed and how it will be paid. If multiple proposals are going to be presented, you might have already added up the total sale and figured the total deposit needed for all ordered items. Whatever means of payment the clients choose—cash, check or credit card—be sure to promptly complete the transaction. Reinforce their decisions by telling the clients how wonderful their choices are and how beautiful the room or rooms will look upon completion. I know you did all the work, but also compliment them on their good taste and ability to quickly and efficiently make decisions. Take this time to explain how and when you expect deliveries to be made. Whether you choose to collect everything in your warehouse for a single large delivery or decide multiple smaller deliveries would be best, the clients need to know the timeline. One more very important part of your sale and presentation will be telling your clients thank you. Don't forget this part of the sale. It's essential that they understand how very much you and your firm appreciate their business and how important they are to your continued success.

Pricing

Once you have created the presentation you want, it must be paired with the budget and the plans for spending the budget. This is where pricing comes into play. As discussed earlier, you will have decided how you markup services and goods, and a consistent approach will help in pricing the products to be included in the presentation. Whether or not you use cost-plus, presented price, or a combination of the two, you should be comfortable with your approach and happy with the profit you expect to make from each segment of the sale. If you are happy with your pricing it will be easier to present the specific costs for each item or portion of the project. This is also where honesty becomes a part of your sales scheme.

If you honestly believe the products or services you are presenting are the right choice for your clients, moving the sale forward will be much easier. And, if you honestly believe the pricing is correct and within your firm's pricing policy guidelines it will be easier for you to ask for and receive the price you present. Without honesty you will constantly watch your back to ensure you don't trip yourself up over the choice or price. Keep it simple and clear. You and your client will be happier and the sales part of interior design will be easier for you.

Proposals

Once the pricing has been established it is important to organize a way to present the costs to the client as you move through the presentation. A proposal is clearly an easy way to have at your fingertips the cost of each service or product presented. The proposal is simply a written summary of what is being offered, how much the total cost to the client will be, and how much deposit is needed to create the sale. I generally create a proposal for each item or service rather than bundle the whole job into one large proposal. It will make it easier to invoice each item when it arrives and is installed if we choose to deliver as the goods are received or services rendered. Within our firm we use a three-part proposal system, which is part of the project management software we employ to manage our clients' orders, deposits, and balances due. One page of the proposal is for the client file, one for the accounting file, and one for clients to keep for their records. There are times, however, when a printed proposal is premature. I might just as easily use a printed worksheet that is filled out in longhand for some presentations and sales. This allows me the flexibility to make changes on the spot to the proposed price should the selection vary from what was originally presented without wasting a lot of clerical time creating proposals that might not be signed. The worksheet is easy to copy, and when clients sign and give me the deposit I am able to send it to my bookkeeping department for printing and accounting. I am also able to very easily give clients a copy until the typed proposal arrives in the mail. This all keeps the accounting in line with our procedures and ensures the client is always aware of pricing and budget status.

Don't Sell Yourself Short

As in all other parts of our profession, meticulous attention to detail is essential to a professional and successful sales technique. This part of your job is not something to shy away from. Successful interior designers across the country are learning more about the art of the sale every day and have incorporated the process into very accomplished and professional interior design firms. Client and project management require a designer be adept at multiple tasks and disciplines. Be forthright in your eagerness to learn all there is to know about selling to your client and managing your business. You're not selling used cars; you're selling dreams. The successful completion of a presentation and sale will bring rewards far beyond superficial monetary benefits. You will relish the pleasure your clients continue to derive from your designs and you will also be pleased when referrals come your way from those same very happy clients.

CHAPTER TEN

ORDERING, FOLLOW-UP, AND PROJECT MANAGEMENT

"Hey, we do a lot more than shipping."
— UPS tag line

As you prepared, presented, and sold to your clients, you considered all the options available as you selected the items you would show. The extent of your library and your relationship with the showrooms and vendors with whom you work also influenced your decisions. Now that the clients have selected the items and services they will incorporate into the project, you will start the ordering process. With this you begin one of the most demanding and time consuming parts of client and project management. For each of the previous components of your relationship with your clients, you have used parts of your skill set related to direct client contact and interaction. Though you should keep your clients informed regarding the progress, they aren't really involved with this particular phase of the project. Keeping them in the loop is essential to good client management and ensuring the project moves forward in an efficient and timely manner. Different skills will be called upon and you will work with vendors, showrooms, and manufacturers more directly during this phase than in any other phase of the client management process.

Who Are All These People?

Depending on the size of the project, you will now be dealing with as many as thirty, forty, or even fifty different people, companies, and vendors. You will have worked with a large portion of this group before on projects for other clients. With many you will have set up open accounts for items ordered, and the process will move very quickly. For some, this might be the first time you have chosen to purchase their particular item or service. These companies will require more attention and will use more of your time and management skills. A third group might include contractors and sub-contractors with whom you will be working but will not be under your direct control. This third group requires a very specialized approach, and you will find they, quite often, require decisions be made in a matter of minutes, unless you have some form of control of the process they implement to move building or construction forward.

The Benefits of a Good Relationship

The companies with whom I have worked in the past and with whom I have established credit accounts are, by far, the easiest group for expediting orders and shipments. We have collaborated over the years in creating a number of projects for clients, and we each know how the other operates. The importance of an open account with these firms can't be stressed enough. Writing checks and waiting for mail to be delivered can slow the process down multiple days, if not weeks. Many firms will not ship until the check has cleared your bank, which could take another three weeks. Through the whole process, that particular part of your project is put on hold. This is not the way to keep a project on time and on budget. An open account with manufacturers will ensure the in-stock items are shipped within a few days to your workroom or office. It also allows you to keep the deposit money in your checking account for at least a month. Cash is important to the efficient operation of any business, and holding on to it as long as possible is an important component to financial stability. There is also another benefit to working with those firms you know and understand—the manufacturer's representative.

A good rep will keep you and your firm apprised of the very latest additions to their line of goods and, when needed, will become your advocate should something go awry during the ordering and delivery process. Working with a professional representative will also help you and the firm work as a team. The relationship should never be adversarial and should, if possible, be congenial and friendly. The rep is not your enemy; he is your stalwart right arm in the war of procurement and production. A good rep will know how your firm operates, understand your ordering process, and be able to help with large and complicated orders. Whether you have a simple fabric order or a complicated sofa with multiple fabrics, trims, and cushioning, your rep will help smooth the way and ensure the order is clear and concise. He or she helps, when needed, to garner quantity discounts or adjustments to multiple orders of the same product. The rep will also keep your library up to date and help purge any items that have been discontinued. A professional manufacturer's representative is clearly interested in your success and the success of his firm. That's the kind of friend you want on your side. Their help is invaluable to the completion of your project and a satisfied client.

New Acquaintances

Working with a showroom, manufacturer, or vendor for the first time presents its own problems. In this case you will not have set up a credit account and the firm with whom you are dealing will not know anything about you or your company. In some instances, it might be appropriate to contact these companies and their representatives as soon as you decide to include an item from their line in your presentation. It will start the ball rolling for creating an open credit account, and you might also want to find out about availability of the particular item you have selected. If they will allow it, you should put these items on reserve for your forthcoming order. Ask them to send along a credit application or, if they are really up to date, deliver it via e-mail to be completed online for a more immediate response. In our office we maintain a completed credit form that contains all the pertinent information needed on most standard credit applications.

Credit References

Hale-Williams Interior Design	Federal Tax ID 44-5588551
25781 Morse Drive	CA Resale # SR GHC 64-551643
Carmel, CA 93923	
831-625-6070 (Phone)	
831-625-6071 (Fax)	
design@hale-williams.com	

Business created February 2000
Operating as a full service residential interior design firm in Maryland since 1987.

Partners: Robert K. Hale, Thomas L. Williams

Brunschwig & Fils
75 Virginia Road
PO Box 905
North White Plains, NY 10603
914-684-5800
Account 2212332

Cowtan & Tout
111 Eighth Ave, Suite 930
New York, NY 10011
212-647-6900
Account 54231

Houles
8584 Melrose Ave.
Los Angeles, CA 90069
310-652-6171
Account 55644

Banking: Valley National Bank of Central California
Attention: Mary Smith
215 Carmel Lane
Carmel, CA 93923
831-624-9221
Account 1212552

Creating credit accounts takes time and, once again, your project will be on hold while your new account is approved. Now would also be a good time to meet the manufacturer's representative if you haven't already. He or she will also be very helpful in moving your credit application along and expediting the order you are placing.

Subs, Mechanics, and Artisans

The third group with which you will deal is often not under your direct control, which could cause problems. Contractors, their sub-contractors, and other artisans are generally under contract with the client, not you or you firm. There are exceptions, but for most interior design firms, the contractor is being paid directly by the client. We work closely with the client and the contractor to ensure each of us has a clear understanding of the role we will play in the project. We have a short letter in which we define each role and we have all the parties sign the agreement to ensure a clear understanding of those roles.

June 12, 2009
Carmel Valley Interior Design
Pro-Build Construction, Inc.
Mr. and Mrs. Jeremy Winters
RE: 25221 SunRise Way, Carmel Valley, CA 93923

The following agreement of understanding between Carmel Valley Interior Design, Pro-Build Construction, Inc., and Mr. and Mrs. Jeremy Winters is prepared to ensure each understands the role of the other during the upcoming remodel.

Mr. and Mrs. Jeremy Winters, hereafter referred to as the client, will contract with, make deposits, and pay additional invoices to Pro-Build Construction, Inc., for the remodel to the residence at 25221 SunRise Way, Carmel Valley, CA 93923. The client will work in coordination with Carmel Valley Interior Design, hereafter referred to as the designer, for all decisions pertaining to the aforementioned remodel. Pro-Build Construction, Inc., hereafter referred to as the contractor, will coordinate all selection requests and plan modifications through the designer.

Using the contractor's finish schedule, the designer, in consultation with the client, will make all design and finish selections and, in writing, update the finish schedule as needed. At no time will the contractor request finish selections or modifications decisions directly from the client. At no time will the client request changes or modifications to the existing finish schedule or remodel plans directly from the contractor.

All parties agree to maintain open and frequent communication as pertains to the remodel and those decisions and selections needed for an efficient and timely completion of the project.

We make it clear from the very beginning that we will be the ultimate voice of the project. We instruct the contractor not to contact the client directly for any decisions. All requests will come through our office and we will work with the client to arrive at the needed decisions. We assure the contractor the decisions will be made quickly and reported back to him or her using our selection form. Yes, we put everything in writing, and so should you.

During the initial phase of the project we would have obtained finish schedules and many of the selections would have been included in the presentation. We never allow the contractor to get ahead of us on selections. His or her job is to complete the building in a timely and cost efficient manner, so there will be little or no time for the contractor to help you with selections. My advice is to make selections early in the project and not have the contractor telephoning on Friday asking for selections that needed to be made last Wednesday. This kind of frantic management creates hard feelings and, ultimately, finger pointing as to who is responsible for the delay of the finished product.

Although the client will see very little of the paperwork and labor involved with order placement and production within your firm, it is imperative there be processes in place that make the ordering, receipt, and warehousing of goods seamless and efficient. In chapter 10 of *Starting Your Career as an Interior Designer* (Allworth Press) I explored the paper trail needed to ensure items are ordered, received, and warehoused efficiently, with a minimum of time required from you or your staff. Within the parameters of client and project management, all of the same tenets still apply. The use of concise and specific three-part purchase orders is required to guarantee items ordered arrive on time and to the address specified. E-mail or telephone follow-up on a weekly basis helps move most orders forward and will also ensure the order is placed with the vendor. Whether mailed, e-mailed, or faxed, a follow-up within five days of ordering keeps everything on track. Keep notes that include who you spoke to, what date and time you spoke, and what the resolution of the conversation or question was. Keep a copy of any e-mails you send or receive that apply to a specific order. Your paper trail is important and helps your firm stay abreast of developments and timing for delivery and installation.

Purchase Order Management

You might also consider using a purchasing service for this kind of procedure. There are a number of services working directly with interior design offices around the country, and the service you select need not be close to your office. Your choice will be predicated on how many purchase orders you send each month, what type of follow-up you want the service to provide, and whether or not you will be paying the invoices for the service. As discussed earlier, outsourcing is a viable and pragmatic choice for a number of the services once kept in house, and it will help you save money and manage your client even more efficiently. Alexandra Gibson of Gibson Design Management offers, among many services, a purchase order outsourcing department. Like all outsourcing, the fee is based on how often the design firm uses the service. There are many benefits to the use of a service like this.

"As a member client of the Gibson Design Management Purchase Order Management Consortium, you and your design firm have access to one source for all your purchasing needs. Additionally, as members you receive the pricing that we receive. You will have the benefit of one centralized location to get all pricing, send all payments, and get reports on all orders. You will be working with a company that has established credit accounts with many showrooms, vendors, and manufacturers. We have a credit history and open accounts that can generally give you preferred pricing. You also have the use of our professional staff to purchase, track, arrange shipment and manage payment for all orders.

Gibson Design Management has taken the concept one step further, with *Six Ways "Teamsourcing" Can Help You Run Your Interior Design Firm Right Now.*

Chances are good that you are not familiar with the term "teamsourcing." While outsourcing professional services is nothing new, we feel the word outsourcing doesn't quite capture the innovative essence of what Gibson Design Management is all about. Our goal is for our member clients to view us as a part of their team. Traditionally, when most people think of outsourcing, there is a lack of personal connection. Our team genuinely feels excited to help our member clients grow and prosper in their businesses. Our member clients are not just clients for whom we process a job.

We've come up with our own official definition of our new word—Webster's hasn't quite caught on yet to our cutting-edge way of thinking. So straight from the "Gibson" dictionary:

teamsourcing (noun)–the innovative, strategic utilization of a fully staffed team of professionals to increase a design firm's efficiency, profitability, expertise, and versatility.

Now that we all understand just what teamsourcing is, let's talk about some of the ways teamsourcing can help you run your interior design business.

Technology

It seems as if the technology realm keeps us constantly feeling out of date and under-equipped. With teamsourcing, the member clients have the benefit of an expert team that is continually learning the latest and greatest, while investing in the necessary equipment to deliver it. The interior designer is able to offer his or her design clients the most up-to-date technology without large expenditures on equipment and training.

Time

The commodity many interior design firms are probably lacking in today's world is time. Try as we might, we haven't figured out how to invent a 30-hour day. However, by teamsourcing some of your responsibilities and tasks, you are able accomplish much more with the 24 hours that *are* in a day. Delegating tasks to a team that can handle them quickly and proficiently allows you the time necessary to focus on the aspects of your business that you enjoy. We can't create more hours in the day, but we can certainly maximize each hour we do have.

Expertise

Let's face it, we can't all be experts at everything. To be honest there are jobs out there I would not enjoy. A major benefit to teamsourcing is the ability to call on specialized teams that have the expertise (and passion) to do what you ask.. Most of us have trained professionals we call on for assistance with at least some of those daily mundane tasks (plumber, electrician, handyman, landscaper, housecleaning, etc.) A gardener and his crew take very good care of your yard! Yes, you are capable of doing it on your own, but it certainly doesn't look nearly as good and takes at least twice as long. Teamsourcing affords a member clients' design firm the advantage of expert teams available to take care of those areas of your business where you lack proficiency and enthusiasm.

Profitability

One of the most significant benefits to teamsourcing is increased profits. With most of our services our member clients can easily markup our service fees and pass them directly onto their clients, making a nice profit. Additionally, you also have those hours available to generate revenue yourself, at your hourly rate. And if you decide you want to celebrate your new profits by taking a trip to the Bahamas, you won't need to worry about keeping an assistant busy. Our team is there when you need us, but is not a financial drain when you don't.

Flexibility

The ability to be nimble, to expand and contract as your projects require, is a huge benefit to teamsourcing. The amount and complexity of projects you are working on is bound to fluctuate. It's never fun to have to turn down a project because you lack the team to handle it or to lay off employees because you lack the work to support them. Teamsourcing gives you the flexibility to handle bigger projects, take a month off in the summer to play with the kids, or redefine yourself as a designer.

Professional Networking

In any business, networking has always been of vital importance. In today's culture it's not just possible, but critical to network with industry contacts around the nation (and beyond). When you teamsource to Gibson Design Management you have the ability to let our social butterflies handle some of the networking for you. We are always connecting with industry affiliates to form and strengthen relationships, keep up on all the latest trends and news, and stay informed about information our members need to know. Our team loves to connect our member clients with industry affiliates and contacts, open doors, and help our members get and stay connected to the interior design industry."

Once you begin to think about the many ways outsourcing can save time and money and you start using those resources, your firm will leap ahead of the competition in terms of client and project management. The intelligent and masterful management of resources of any kind is a skill at which professional interior designers will become more adept as we move forward in this new century. Why not jump on the bandwagon now and get your "team" ready for the challenges ahead?

Make New Friends, But Keep the Old

Terry McLaughlin is a sales representative for a major international fabric house and has worked in that position for over two years. Prior to his current position he was a sales representative for a semi-custom window treatment company. Terry has also managed an interior design firm overseeing six designers and two assistants. As you will see, the job of manufacturer's representative is multi-faceted.

"I believe it is very important to build positive, healthy relationships with manufacturers' representatives whether they are showroom salespeople, territory representatives, showroom managers, or even the librarian who pulls your samples. These people are here to help you in the design process and assist in selecting products for your clients. Just as you want to build a great relationship with your client, these professionals want to build a great relationship with you. It is their goal to help you select the right product for your clients, answer any questions, and ultimately place an order with their particular firm.

As I think about the designers I call on, I can say that I have a great professional relationship with all. I truly can put myself in their shoes because I have done their job. I have met with clients, presented a scheme, and had it rejected. I have ordered fabric only to find out it has been discontinued or would take months to get. Unfortunately, these things happen. It's how you, as a designer, handle these challenges with your representatives that can make or break a relationship. If you are organized, communicate on a professional level, and have a bit of understanding for your sales reps, you will have a great relationship.

What Will You Have?

The ordering process starts with the first client meeting, when you explore what will be needed for the particular project. You will figure out a plan of action as far as product, budget, and timeframe. These are all important things to think about as you are selecting items to show your client. I'll use shopping for fabric as an example of the process.

You, as a designer, can shop for fabric in a number of different ways. You might visit the showroom, meet with an "outside" sales rep, or even the visit the company's Web site.

When visiting a showroom, you will be overwhelmed with choices. Most have thousands of fabrics on display. Multiply that by the hundreds of fabric houses and you will *really* be overwhelmed. Getting the "lay of the land," therefore, is very important. The first thing to do when you visit a showroom for the first time is to ask how it's laid out. There is actually a method to the way the items are displayed. I enjoy taking the time to show designers around our showroom because it will make future visits more efficient for them. Another smart thing to do is to ask an associate where a particular type of fabric is. He or she can quickly point you in the right direction rather than leaving you to search aimlessly.

You will also be contacted by your territory sales, or outside sales, rep. This professional is also a good person to know. Typically it is the outside sales rep's job to present the newest collections from the manufacturer, bring you products you might be shopping for, or simply to act as another contact with the company. As an outside rep myself, I cover a large territory and am able to meet with many people who might not make it to our showroom very often. I also meet with firms that are a few blocks away from our showroom, because it is easier and more time efficient for everyone on staff to see a number of new products in one sitting.

Sometimes I have designers tell me that they will look at new products when they visit the showroom. That is all well and good, but most of the time, the designer is on a specific mission when visiting showrooms and won't take the time to review new products. Staying on top of what is new within the industry is critical. Don't discount the importance of meeting with your reps to see new products and review updated colors and styles. If you don't have a studio, you can typically set up an appointment in the showroom to see the new products. If you know you are going to meet with your outside rep, let him or her know what kinds of projects you are working on and if he or she can shop for you. This saves you a lot of time by having choices brought to you. It is great when designers find products during a showing because the selection represents the newest options for their client, meaning they're usually in stock. I also serve as a contact to the showroom so I am able to process orders, answer questions, help with customer service issues, or just about anything else you can throw my way.

On the Web

Lastly, most companies have a Web site where you can shop for products, look at technical information, and even get pricing. Many designers use these tools to their advantage. It helps to get a sense of what's available and helps you to "pre-shop" before coming into the showroom. And, since the site is available twenty-four hours a day, seven days a week, you can shop at any time. Some Web sites will let you order samples directly and even place orders. After finding your selection, you should check stock and prices *before* presenting it to the client. A lot of designers skip this step, and it can be a costly mistake. I've worked with designers who have presented a fabric to the client and had them buy in only to find out it is discontinued or it has a long backorder. Once you have sold a fabric to clients, it is harder to sell a different one to them because they will have that first fabric in mind! You can check pricing and stock by calling the showroom, faxing, e-mailing, and even checking the vendor Web site. Once you know the fabric is available and within the budget, you should present it. If, for some reason, the fabric is not available ask the rep to shop for an alternate. Also, please wait to order a fabric until it has been presented to the client, unless there is limited stock. Many designers will reserve several different fabrics before presenting it to their client. This process ties up thousands of dollars of unneeded fabric for weeks. As mom always said, "Take only what you need." That definitely holds true when ordering.

Tracking

When you place your order, you can place a reserve on the fabric, typically for two weeks. This gives you time to have the client sign off and to pay for the product. It is your job as a designer to stay on top of this timeframe. Either write it on a calendar or tell your assistant to follow-up. From time to time I've seen designers lose a reserve and then get bent out of shape because they "didn't know" it was going to expire. Showrooms will try to place a courtesy reminder call but it should not be expected of the vendor. In some cases, you may be able to extend the reserve for a bit more time. This is probably the most frustrating thing for me to see because I know designers are making it hard for themselves. They jump the gun and place the reserve when the client hasn't even signed off on the purchase. It is important to follow the orders through the process and make sure that you are aware of your reserves.

You also will have the option of asking for a cutting for approval. This is a piece of the actual fabric from the dye lot that you have ordered. It is good to ask for it but not always necessary. It helps you ensure you are receiving the correct fabric and that the color will be true to what was presented. Keep in mind that most cotton and linen fabrics will be slightly different from dye lot to dye lot, which you should explain to the client ahead of time. Once you have received the CFA, you must approve it in a timely manner to ensure the reserve doesn't expire. Some designers present the

CFA to their client for approval. Quite honestly, I think this is an unnecessary step that only drags the process on. The client should trust that as long as you've seen the CFA and it looks good, the order is a go.

You may run into a situation in which the product is out of stock. Vendors try to have as much stock available as they believe will be ordered but sometimes it is just not possible due to supply and demand. If there is a backorder, we will try to advise you of an accurate timeframe. Many designers do not understand why it can take six, eight, or ten weeks, or even longer to produce a fabric. The mills work on a rotation of what they produce, the looms have to be set, and the proper threads placed. Sometimes they may be producing runs of velvet before they move onto chenille. The vendors cannot necessarily control this. Another thing to remember is that most European companies take a month-long holiday during July or August. This obviously affects production and delivery. Again, prepare the client ahead of time for possible backorders. We will often advise a designer who is on a time crunch to not select a backordered fabric.

Many vendors no longer stock products but work with mills that keep products in stock. This is becoming more commonplace in the industry and it is called cut yardage goods. Basically, an order is placed and the mill will confirm that they have stock. A CFA may or may not be available. Typically, full payment will be required as the product is shipping directly from the mill. Keep in mind the shipping timeframe may take a bit longer if the product is shipping from Europe or Asia.

When ordering your product, try to give as much information at the time of ordering as possible. This includes accurate yardage, proper side mark, and delivery address. Quite often designers will place a reserve for fabric and then need to increase or reduce the yardage based on the workroom's requirements. It is best to order more yardage than necessary and reduce it versus trying to add more. The proper side mark information ensures the fabric doesn't get misplaced or misused by your workroom. Finally, the proper shipping address is needed. We have run into situations in which a designer gives the wrong address and we have to explain trying to get product rerouted during shipping is not an easy process and at times cannot be done.

I'd Like a Purchase Order, Please

It is best to place your order with a purchase order, which identifies the product, quantity, side mark, and shipping address. It will make everyone's lives much easier to have the information upfront. These can be handwritten or computer generated. The more organized and professional designers use these religiously and there is rarely any confusion with their orders.

Most vendors ship everyday and use ground service or freight companies to ship their goods. Be aware that there will be shipping and handling costs in addition to the price of the goods you order. Make sure that you are charging your client for these additional costs or it will cost YOU money. Some vendors will ship without collecting shipping costs up front while others will hold an order until all monies have been collected. Please do not take it out on the company's staff if you are charged for additional shipping costs. We do not control it at our level. These charges are often based on weight of goods, packaging, and destination. If you do not agree with a charge, there is usually an associate on the corporate level who can help you ascertain exactly what the charges should be. Everyone gets in a pinch sometimes, and if you prefer shipping via overnight or second day, at YOUR expense, most companies are happy to comply.

I guess the best thing that I can say about building a relationship with your manufacturer's rep and showroom personnel is the Golden Rule, "Do unto others as you would have them do unto you." If you are kind to the people with whom you come in contact, they will be kind to you. We all want to help you sell products to your client, but sometimes issues will arise. Remember that you are dealing with a person who is your advocate to get the problem solved. He or she may not have the answer immediately, so calling repeatedly won't help. You also may not like the answer or solution that is proposed. But keep in mind that you will be dealing with this person again, so you should act professionally and voice your feedback in a respectful way. I have heard horror stories of designers yelling, hanging up the phone, and even using profanities when things don't go their way.

As in life, you will get along with some people better than others. That's okay. You need to be professional, however, with anyone you encounter. As a rep, I am lucky to encounter many diverse and talented designers. I truly respect everyone for choosing this profession. It is not as easy as it looks. And the great designers make it look effortless. They have a lot of help behind the scenes, which includes their staff, delivery people, artisans, craftspeople, and hopefully, their vendors."

Brunschwig, We Have a Problem

As stated earlier in this chapter the vendors with whom you have worked before will be the easiest and quickest to facilitate an order. That doesn't mean, however, that strict follow-up isn't required. As with any order, weekly calls and notes on how the order is progressing will ultimately ensure a clean and trouble-free receipt of goods. With these vendors you will also probably have a more genial and friendly relationship with the manufacturer's representative. He or she will be there for you should something go awry with the order. These professionals are interested in your business and whether or not you order from their firm.

As you work with them you will develop a relationship that will be of great value should there be any sort of problem with ordering or receiving the goods. This will help maintain the contact needed to ensure goods are delivered on time and on budget. If you have some sort of problem, don't get on the phone and start screaming at the rep or showroom manager. Remember, you have been doing business with these people for a long time and they really do want to help. Explain the problem in a calm and unexcited voice. Be ready to offer what you believe will be a fair and equitable solution. If the wrong fabric was sent, they will replace it. If there is a nick on the cocktail table, they will work with you to have it repaired. Once a solution has been reached be sure to thank them for their help. Be sure, also, to let the representative know when goods arrive on time, in good condition, and exactly as ordered. By expressing respect for the contacts with whom you work in every area of your business, you create and maintain a team that will bend over backwards to give you what you need when you need it. Mutual respect ensures an open and honest dialogue, and you will be listened to when there is a problem. All of this helps you manage your clients and projects without unneeded drama.

CHAPTER ELEVEN
DELIVERY AND PLACEMENT

"Opportunity is missed by most people because it is dressed in overalls and looks like work."
— Thomas Edison

Everything is ordered and you are ready for all the items to be placed in your client's home. But wait, there is so much more going on behind the scenes before you can even think about getting everything out to your client. For most furniture pieces you are going to need a warehouse and receiving facility to receive, unpack, inspect, and store each piece you have ordered. The drapery workroom will be ready to deliver shortly, the wall covering you ordered is in-house, and the painter is still days away from finishing the trim in most of the rooms. Invoices need to be prepared and you must decide whether or not to deliver in stages or all at once. The clients will need to be notified about delivery dates and times, and you will need to clear your schedule to attend the delivery. You thought this was going to be easy, didn't you? Guess again. As with restaurants and hotels, what goes on "back of the house" is what really separates the pros from the wannabes when it comes to client and project management. This also gives you and your firm a wonderful opportunity to demonstrate your ability as managers. Throughout the process of delivery and placement, attention to detail and a strict adherence to the systems your firm has in place will speak volumes to your clients. They should see a seamless and worry-free installation and not be aware of how much goes on behind the scenes.

Organize, Organize, Organize

Not only is a delivery hard work physically, the organization that goes into any delivery also requires each member of your office to be trained and mentally prepared. The people with whom you will be working outside the office have very important roles to play, as well. Each individual vendor, workroom, or mechanic should be organized, professional, and reliable enough to help you maintain strict control over the final product. It is up to you and your firm to set the parameters as to what happens and when it happens to complete the project in a timely manner. Usually the firms you select to create the drapery you design, the furniture you select, and the finishes used in the project are known to you and understand your requirements and processes. If not, prepare a written description of exactly what is expected from anyone you've not worked with before. I have a minimum level of finish when it comes to drapery. All of my drapery must be fabricated using a matching cotton thread only. All drapery panels must have a minimum of two and one half times fullness. Hems and headers must be triple folded. There are other specific items within my work orders, and when working with a known drapery workroom, the employees are aware of our needs and adhere to our construction requirements. You must ensure that new firms understand your needs. This may require one or more meetings that will not be needed on future projects. Make sure you factor in the extra time to ensure timely delivery.

Tracking the Orders

The work your firm does to prepare for the upcoming delivery is also very important. Once the orders are placed there should be a system within your office that tracks the status of each order, allowing for almost constant updates. Depending on the size of the project and the amount of orders that have been placed, timing will become more and more critical. Some items need not be ordered as early as others. Similar to what is called "triage" in the medical profession, you will select those items needing the most immediate attention first and slowly go through the list to those items that will not be ordered for some weeks or even months. Your firm will also need to have an update system in place that calls for weekly updates and, as you get closer to delivery time, daily updates. Make sure your needs are heard by your vendors loud and clear. Whether you telephone or e-mail your vendors or workrooms, do it in a professional and calm manner. If there is a delay, try to define when the item will be ready to ship. You should also explore shipping alternatives in case a quick delivery of the product is necessary as you approach the delivery date. Keep scrupulous notes about whom you have talked with, the date and time of conversations, and what decisions were made regarding shipment. Until all of these items are delivered, a constant track of their status will ensure a prompt and efficient delivery.

Whether your plan is to deliver all at once or as goods arrive, you need to be aware of the status of any construction or remodeling that is taking place. You don't want items standing around a warehouse or your office because they were ordered too early and can't be delivered. At the same time you don't want to be running around frantically trying to get items shipped that were ordered too late. Maintaining strict control of when and how items arrive helps manage the project and your client.

Warehousing and Storage

One of the most important decisions you will make for your firm is where to receive and store furniture before delivery and who will ultimately deliver those goods. If you are in the very enviable position of having the space and staff to have everything delivered to your facility, so much the better. Strict control over this part of the client management process is very important, and having everything in-house helps you maintain that control. If, on the other hand, you will be employing the services of an outside firm for receipt and delivery there are a few things to look for.

In most areas of the country there are moving and storage companies willing to perform this service for you. Be aware, however, of exactly what they will provide. Some are connected to national moving company chains and have little, if any, direct interest in interior designers and their particular set of challenges. Residential interior designers, as a group, tend to order small quantities of very expensive items that usually need special attention and storage. Receiving and warehousing firms that do specialize in receiving and inspecting deliveries for interior designers may not be in your particular area. Be very selective and particular about the facility you ultimately choose for your furniture storage. Make an appointment to inspect the facility with the manager or owner before you send anything to them. You will be looking for a number of things. How clean is the warehouse? Is there a dedicated space for interior designer goods? Who is the person in charge of that particular area? Make sure to meet the designer-area manager and ask about the process of receipt and inspection of goods. Are the items completely opened and inspected before being rewrapped and stored? What happens if there is freight damage? Who within the organization will initiate the freight claim, and when and how will your office be notified? The items this firm will be handling on your behalf are generally very expensive and delicate, with fine fabrics and finishes that need special attention. If the company you're talking to doesn't understand the need for very precise and specific controls, keep looking.

Beyond Storage and Delivery

One very important service moving and storage companies offer is a site inspection to ensure all the pieces you are ordering can be delivered to the site and room you specify. Remember the sofa you ordered that was just too long to go around the doorway into the study for that client who simply had to have the larger piece? What about the buffet that was too long to go into the freight elevator in the high-rise condominium building on the Upper East Side? We have all had those mistakes crop up while delivering pieces we have ordered. One of the best ways to avoid this problem is to preview the site with your delivery company. To these professionals it will become evident very quickly whether or not the items you are about to order will fit through, around, or in the various openings, elevators, or stairways that might impede the efficient delivery of your clients' new furnishings. They will also be able to define for you the maximum sizes of items to be ordered. Knowing ahead of time what will or won't fit is very important. The challenges for designers in large cities are different from those in rural areas, but each still needs to ensure the delivery can happen without having to cut the sofa in half or take doors off hinges.

Sally Cardinale, of Cardinale Moving and Storage in Castroville, California, owns one of the best interior-designer-specific warehouse and storage facilities. Her firm's main focus is short and long-haul moving of households but they have a dedicated area for interior designer receipt and storage.

"Cardinale Moving & Storage is a family business, locally owned and operated by the Cardinale family since 1972. We pride ourselves on maintaining permanent relationships with our customers by providing outstanding service, move after move, with no exceptions.

We handle receiving, storage, and delivery installations for approximately fifty interior designers. Most of these designers are located on the Monterey Peninsula, but more than a dozen are located in other states. In addition to these clients, we are the furniture mover of choice for the Park Hyatt Highlands Inn, Quail Lodge, Hyatt Regency-Monterey, and the Monterey Marriott.

Our receiving procedures are fairly straightforward. We open and inspect all items while the freight drivers are still at our location. If there are significant damages that we feel are beyond repair, we notify the interior designer immediately and get his or her permission to refuse the delivery. If we cannot reach the designer we will refuse the delivery if we feel that is the best course of action. If we feel the item is repairable, we will still contact the designer, mark the damages on the freight bill, and file a freight claim on behalf of the interior design firm. If the freight driver refuses to wait, which is often the case, we mark that on the freight bill and contact the freight company if there are damages. If the delivery cartons and/or crates are the best way to store the items, they will be stored in their original containers. If not, we will cloth-pad wrap each item. We will then place the items in our storage containers, which are large wooden storage vaults. Each item is individually tagged with our receiving number, the interior design firm's name, the client's name, purchase order number, and the room location for the piece. We can locate each piece, on paper, at a moment's notice, but we need at least 24-hours advance notice to physically access an item. Sofas would not be put in the vaults, but wrapped in plastic shrink wrap and placed on our sofa racks in the warehouse. Any extraordinarily large items (those that would not fit in a vault) like armoires or large chandeliers would also be cloth padded and set in our designer overflow area.

Depending on the type of delivery and delivery access, the items will be delivered to the residence in the storage vaults on flat bed trailers or off-loaded onto a covered van. There are many variables surrounding each delivery type."

A professional firm is going to help make your client management easier by making receiving, storage, and delivery clean and worry-free. Well, almost. Good communication between you and your warehouse will also help to maintain the quality needed for this part of the operation. Issue purchase orders for every delivery you expect to be sent to your warehouse of choice. On the purchase order, specify the items to be received, who will be sending them, the quantity, the finish, and the types of pieces. The "tag" line should include your firm's name, the client name, item purchase order number, and the room to which the piece will eventually be delivered. All of these details are important, and this quality service is not cheap. When you first start looking for a warehouse, be wary of anyone telling you he or she can do it for less. Take a hard long look at what you will and will not get when going this route. This is an area in which a little more money spent on professional services will make the final product worthy of your firm's name and reputation.

Cover That Window

The delivery and installation of window coverings is another area in which expertise and experience are important for successful completion. Our firm has always worked with drapery workrooms that employ their own installers who are also responsible for the check measure taken before any work begins on the drapery. We do a quick measure of the windows we expect to cover and work out a quote request using our measurements. Our workroom employees understand there might be small variances in the measurements when we place the order, but this first request is intended to get the job moving. Once the client has ordered the drapery, we ask for the check measure to be made. We are always on site when the measure occurs in case there are any questions about where we want panels, valances, shades, or any other part of the completed window covering.

Once the window coverings are ready for delivery and installation we meet the installer on site and make sure everything is as it should be. The workroom is instructed to pack the window coverings in a way that ensures no creases or unexpected snags during shipping to the site. If at all possible we move the client away from the area in which the installation takes place. Clients watching every part of the installation can become anxious about the final result and might not completely understand the process and what is required to install large and complicated window treatments. The installer will be drilling holes in walls, mounting support brackets, and, in general, creating controlled chaos until finished with the installation. Once the drapery is in place the installer should steam the drapery panels and valances to smooth out any creases or wrinkles that might have appeared during shipping. There are also chemical sprays that achieve the same thing as steaming—ensure this particular step is included with any installation of fine drapery. A complete clean-up of the area around the installation is an important final step before presenting the finished product to your client.

Wall Coverings

Whether painting the walls, creating stylish glazed finishes, or wallpapering, the installation of these items requires planning and preparation. Your firm must decide at what point to install any or all of the types of finishes chosen. Finding and working with a qualified professional, called a mechanic, requires numerous interviews and inspections of completed jobs to ascertain who will be the best fit for you and your firm. These professionals should understand your need for estimates that will come in on time and on budget. You will be staging their work prior to the delivery of furniture and fittings, and any delay will cost you and your client money. As with most deliveries and installations I don't suggest the client be around for the event. Painting is one of the hardest for them to witness. As the painter begins to cover the walls, clients might say the color is not the one they chose. Until the painting is finished and dry, no one can precisely define how the paint will look. For one thing the new color is going over an older color. In most instances the two colors will not be compatible and the first coat generally does not cover completely. There will be bleed-through and the contrast of the two colors or shades will affect the look of the new color. All in all, this is not what you want your clients to see. As a matter of fact, painting one small area or even a whole wall with a new color to determine whether or not it is the right shade is a terrible way to decide on colors in a room. The reflected light from one shade to another will affect both shades. As a professional you should have the ability to suggest the correct color and shade for a particular space and be confident in your choice. Using larger samples for most of your design scheme selections will further enhance your ability to choose correctly.

Glazed walls, whether high-end, French-style plaster finishes, or a simple sponged wash, require a more talented and creative professional than simple painting. Many painters, of course, claim the ability to create sophisticated glazed finishes and some actually do have the talent. Most, however, simply don't care or do not have the ability needed for these types of finishes. All of these finishes begin with a painted wall and some glazing professionals don't do that part of the job. Once again, your office will define what is needed and who comes in first to create the glazed wall you have proposed. These finishes are far more time consuming than a simple two-coat paint job and, of course, more expensive. Don't shy away from talented professionals because of expense. You want this finish to be right the first time. It should have wonderful nuances in tone and shade appearance to be truly successful. Your clients and you will be far happier with a professional who may appear at the onset to be more expensive but is able to achieve your goals in an efficient manner with little fuss.

Wallpaper

As a tool for a first-rate interior designer, wallpaper can't be beat. I don't mean those $9.99 per roll, self-adhesive pieces of junk found at paint and paper stores, though. I'm talking about quality designer papers found at all the nation's leading design showrooms. These companies have been dealing with wallpaper for years and know what does and does not work. I have always spent a lot of time educating my clients about the different types of wallpaper available and how each contributes to the finished design. Beautiful, hand-screened papers are still among my favorites. With upwards of fifteen and sometimes twenty-four color screens, these papers have a texture not found in any other type of finish for walls. Most of the designs used for these papers are unique to the manufacturer and have been created by some of the most talented designers in our industry. Definitely not what your grandmother had on her powder room walls. These papers are stylish and up-to-date.

Whether using this type of paper, a contemporary expanded vinyl, or lush grasscloth, the person in charge of hanging the paper should be an experienced and talented professional. He or she should know a lot about how wallpaper is manufactured and what types of adhesive are the most effective for each different type of paper. Remember that before the wallpaper can be hung, the walls must be prepared. For many, many years the best foundation for the application of wallpaper has been an oil-based enamel paint or a specific wallpaper base. This finish seals the wall and allows the wallpaper paste to go on smoothly. Many people complain about the inability to remove wallpaper once it's hung. A good sealer will eliminate that problem. By sealing the wall, the paper has only the adhesive to hang on to and will leave the wall clean and clear when it is removed. The sealer actually makes removal easier and less messy than when not applied. Your wallpaper professional will also understand how to get the most out of the paper you supply for the job. There is always some waste, but you want it kept to a minimum. Clean tools, neat practices, and the constant replacement of razor blades are what separate the professional wallpaper installer from others in the trade. The application of wallpaper is very labor intensive and even a small powder room will probably take up to two days to complete. There are a couple of reasons why. First, once paste has been applied to the paper it should rest. Sounds silly, I know, but the paper should be folded on itself and allowed to adjust to the moisture and weight of the paste. In this stage, in which the paper is "booked," the resting allows the paper to expand. This ensures that once it's on the wall it won't pull or wrinkle. The second reason wallpaper takes a while to install is the need to trim many high-end papers. These papers arrive from the manufacturer with a small edge, or selvedge, that shows the register marks from the printing process. This needs to be removed prior to hanging. The use of a long straight edge for clean cutting is imperative. A crisp and clean joining of paper panels is essential. As with all types of installation, proper clean-up makes the finished product look so much better.

Floors and Floor Coverings

If you have chosen to specify hard surface flooring of any type and will be responsible for procuring the materials, a professional mechanic is essential to the overall quality of the job. The individual actually doing the job should be the one to measure and specify exactly how much material will be required. There is always a little overage with this type of material, but excessive waste is not good for you or your client and should be avoided. If your mechanic continually has you order too much material, consider changing mechanics. The mechanic should also have a warehouse for storage until the installation will occur. With hardwood it is usually important for the material to be stored in the space in which it will be installed to adapt to the specific humidity of the space. This allows contraction and expansion to occur before the hardwood is installed. Be sure to factor in this time requirement when you order. Also bear in mind where and how the hardwood will be stored in the space. You don't want painters, carpenters, or paper hangers working around this very valuable material.

Your carpet and rug installer does far more than roll out an area rug over a pad for you and your clients. These professionals will measure rooms for carpeting and help you decide which type of padding is appropriate for the space. While the space is being measured you will decide the direction in which the carpet will run when laid. When ordering twelve-foot-wide goods the placement of the seams will be critical to a professional finish. Generally the seam should not be in the center of the space. The largest width is usually placed in the center of the space with the smaller widths on either side. Once again, this makes for a cleaner finish. Quite often the installer also stocks padding, so you won't have to order that when ordering the carpet. Once they are ordered, the flooring specialist will receive and warehouse the goods until your client's space is ready for installation.

Generally, carpet installation takes place after the painting or paper hanging is finished. There are those who would argue the paint might get scuffed or chipped by installers. Good installers will do their best to avoid that, and if a nick were to occur, the installer will have the painter come back to touch up the area. Professional installers are neat and tidy, treat the carpet with care, and understand that each type of carpet requires a different installation technique. Some narrow-width carpets require seaming with a needle to lie properly. Most man-made products, however, employ a tape and heat system to keep seams closed and the carpet flat. Carpets with patterns and repeats require more sophisticated types of measurement and installation. A professional carpet warehouse will adjust to the changing needs of the product selected. The men and women who install carpet and lay rugs should always be aware of their surroundings and careful while in your client's home or office. Many remove their shoes while on the job and always clear their debris before leaving the site. Once the carpet or rug is installed, a thorough vacuuming is necessary to ensure the product is flat, seamed properly, and aligned to match any pattern or texture.

Cabinetry

Built-in cabinets, whether in the kitchen, bath, or family room, require the services of a qualified installer or contractor. Generally the cost of installation is above the cost of fabrication, and many craftsmen and women will not deal with the installation. You, therefore, are responsible to find another person to accomplish the installation. In this particular instance it would be a good idea to use the services of your strategic alliance partners in the building or contracting world. This is, after all, what they do for a living. Arrange for the cabinets to be as close to finished as possible at the workshop before delivery to the site. Have your contractor pick them up, deliver them to the site, and install. If necessary, your painter may have to come and do any last minute touch-ups that might be required. From the clients' point of view this, too, is a seamless installation and they will not really be aware of how many people are involved with this type of installation.

All or Nothing at All

Shirli Yazaki of SYI Design, LLC, in Glendale, California, specializes in residential projects ranging from pre-construction planning and the design phase to fully furnished and accessorized interiors. Shirli is an allied member of ASID, NKBA, and BPN. Her experience in partial and complete deliveries is very helpful.

"Finally the time has come, and the item you ordered is ready to be shipped or picked up (will call) for placement at your client's. For merchandise such as case goods, chairs, upholstered items, and large accessories, the vendor will ship through a common carrier to a delivery service. The delivery company serves as a partner to transport the merchandise and correctly place it in the client's home in the best possible condition. In most cases it's important to utilize the services of a reputable white glove delivery service. This service may be more expensive, but in the long run will save the designer possible headaches. The reasons are as follows:

- The delivery service will inspect the shipment before the bill of lading is signed for acceptance and will take appropriate action if there are any damages. All damages are notated and claims are filed with the shipper and vendor. In most cases the delivery service has personnel who can do some repairs but will also notify the designer of the situation. If something is beyond local repair, the delivery service will work with the designer and vendor to resolve the problem.

The service will hold merchandise in safe storage if the designer wants to stage a single delivery day. There maybe a time limit for holding goods and a warehousing charge if the time limit is exceeded. The number of men scheduled for installation depends on the weight and bulk of items to be delivered and the ease of getting them from the truck to the job site. The designer must inform the delivery service if any steps are involved or if the job site is on the 2nd floor.

- The company will provide a quote based on client location, ease of delivery process, number of items involved, and number of men required.

- The personnel are usually dressed in company shirts with their names embroidered.

- The company name is on the transportation truck.

- They inspect the path from the truck to the desired location and move any objects that might impede the delivery process.

- Applicable items are delivered wrapped in blankets to avoid damage to the item itself and to the property of the client.

- They perform simple assembly of merchandise either before delivery or at the job site.

- They take every precaution not to soil items during the installation process.

- Employees are knowledgeable about the correct procedure of laying an area rug and corresponding pad.

- They will place items in the correct location according to the designer space plan and will not have an attitude if something has to be moved from the original location.

- They will remove all cartons and package wrappings from the items and will take it with them.

- They will ensure items are delivered in good condition and they often can repair on the job site. Before they leave the premises, the designer or client will sign a release form and should note either that everything is in good condition or any problems. At this point the designer is responsible for taking care of any problems. It is the prerogative of the designer, however, to accept or reject an item. The delivery service is responsible for addressing any issues.

- They will lightly clean and dust the merchandise.

- They will leave the job only after everything is finished to the satisfaction of the designer and client.

Client and Delivery

Designers should inform their clients at the time of purchase that there will be a delivery and placement charge apart from the inbound freight charges. This avoids any misunderstandings when the time comes to pay the delivery service, which in many cases can run several hundred dollars. The designer can either bill the client for this service or allow the client to pay directly. I prefer for the client to pay the service directly at the time of delivery and charge for my time to stage the delivery. In this way clients do not feel they are paying the designer twice for getting the merchandise to them. For the first delivery, the designer should explain the value of the delivery service to the clients so they have an understanding of the charges involved. If the clients don't tip the delivery men, I will take care of that. They usually deserve it, and the next time I work with them I will receive even better service. The designer also needs to refer to their state's tax regulations and charge accordingly. For instance, in the state of California the designer is required to charge sales tax on the time charged to the client for picking up an item and delivering it to the client.

The best situation is for the designer to be present when merchandise is delivered. The designer is familiar with the space plan and can make the best decisions if adjustments need to be made. When the time comes to inspect the merchandise the designer will be the most able to make sure everything is in good condition. This may include determining if doors are hung straight, drawers operate smoothly, shelving is installed properly, furniture legs don't wobble on the flooring, sectionals are connected properly, there are no scratches or dings, and dealing with any other possible challenges to a clean delivery. The client is relying on the designer's knowledge and ability to ensure that what is delivered is in good condition. The designer sometimes has to step in when clients are too picky and explain why something is acceptable. During this process, clients start to gain genuine confidence in their designer and appreciate his or her expertise and ability to create beautiful and functional interiors that are just for them.

Pros of Staging a Single Delivery Day

- The room(s) is immediately transformed and the client sees the total effect of all the planning and work at one time.

- The design quickly impacts the life of the client. The client may move forward on other projects earlier based on the results.

- The client sees the designer not only as creative, but also as an efficient business manager.

- The client will save shipping and delivery charges if multiple items are purchased from the same source.

- Single day delivery charge will be less than multiple ones.

Cons of Staging a Single Delivery Day

- God forbid the clients change their minds on the direction of the design and everything has already been purchased. Designers should always maintain in their records signed proposals or invoices from the clients. Then the designer needs to work with the client to salvage the situation quickly.

- The clients can't pay for all the balances and delivery charges in a relatively short time. Designers should provide their clients with a monthly statement of invoices paid and the balance due to avoid an embarrassing situation in the future.

Pros of Small Deliveries

- Clients feel that all monies aren't being committed at one time. They have an opportunity to budget accordingly.

- Designers can see how the overall design of the room is progressing and make adjustments if needed.

> ### Cons of Small Deliveries
>
> - It takes longer to finish a project.
> - Clients will spend more money on multiple deliveries."

I Want to Hold Your Hand

Delivery and placement is such an important part of client and project management that it should also be a part of your marketing and promotion campaign. Clients like to feel as if they are your only concern when deliveries take place. Sharing the excitement of the new furnishings and reinforcing the soundness of their choices helps ensure they are happy with the space the two of you have created. This type of hand-holding is important for good word of mouth as well as client relations. Whether or not you also choose to mention delivery and placement in your advertising and promotional pieces is up to you. Most interior design firms don't emphasize this part of our process and you might be able to set your firm apart from the others by highlighting this very important component.

As with each phase of the design process we've discussed so far, communication about the delivery and placement process with your clients will keep them in the loop and excited about the process. Far too many interior designers overlook or ignore this phase of client management. Now is not the time to disappear from view. Clients want to know you are interested in how the space ultimately looks and your presence at a delivery is vital to building and maintaining a great clientele.

CHAPTER TWELVE
A CLIENT FOR LIFE

"Forever is composed of nows."
– Emily Dickinson (1830–1886)

You have now discovered who your optimum clients are and how to reach out to them. They called and asked you to come to the proposed project site for a meeting. A contract was signed and they liked what you presented. The time between ordering and delivery went smoothly and the delivery was a piece of cake. As an accomplished client and project manager you have succeeded in orchestrating a seamless process for all participants. Your clients have told you again and again how pleased they are, and the return surveys have supported their praise. How, then, can you ensure these clients come back to you for future projects? This, of course, is the sixty-four-thousand-dollar question. Well, it might be more like one-hundred-thousand-dollars, but you get the idea. Maintaining a client during the project is, as you have seen, an exact process and requires the design team be detail-oriented and willing to work with the client to achieve the best possible outcome. At this point in the process, you must be ready to close the books and move on. Don't let the project drag on with minor repairs, deliveries, and tedious follow-up from your office. Make sure everyone understands all items under the scope of the project have been completed and the project has come to a close. This is not necessarily a bad time, but you may be surprised to know both clients and designers sometimes feel sadness at the completion of a successful project. Post-project depression can sometimes create a feeling of emptiness where there should be excitement and a sense of accomplishment. Now is not the time, however, to simply fold your tent and walk away. To maintain clients' loyalty the design firm should continue to include the clients in the activities of the principals and associates. Understanding how to accomplish that is part of the ongoing process of client retention. First, though, a little bit of follow-up might be necessary to finish the project.

That's Not What I Ordered

Wrapping up a project can be very complex. No matter how precise you are with ordering, receiving, and delivery, there will inevitably be differences between what you ordered and what is delivered. In most instances you will be able to rectify the problem quickly and with a minimum of fuss. In fact, good client management requires an almost instant resolution of any little challenges that may arise in any project. You and your team should always be ready to face these disputes head on and with an optimistic and supportive attitude. Even though everything we do for our clients is special order and they have signed a proposal stating they understand what is to be ordered, there will, from time to time, be discrepancies. It can be as simple as a question of shading on a particular fabric used for pillows and as major as a complete dislike of seating ordered for a whole room. That happened to me once.

For a smaller-scaled room I was designing, we specified a sofa, two chairs, and matching tables. The scale of the pieces was most appropriate to the space. The style, a bamboo frame, wrapped in leather, with fully-upholstered seating, was just right for the tone of the area. It was even going to come in under budget. Both the husband and wife approved the purchase and it was delivered on time. The client accepted delivery and signed that she was satisfied with the items delivered. I had no sooner gotten back to the office when she called to say her husband simply could not stand the smaller scale, wanted the furniture removed as soon as possible, and a new selection made quickly for delivery as soon as we could organize it. I asked her to give me a few minutes to organize with my team and decide what could be done, and I would phone her back within the next two hours. First, I had to decide what options there were for seating in the same space. In the concept phase I had shown the couple a larger-scaled, fully-upholstered sofa and chairs, and I decided to show that again. I also made arrangements for the recently delivered furniture to be picked up the following morning. I phoned the client, asked that she and her husband come into the office at their earliest convenience, and said I would show them options.

The next morning the furniture was removed, and the following day the clients came into the office. I showed them how the larger-scale furniture I had reselected for them would impact the area in question and they decided to go with it anyway. As it turned out, I took back the special-ordered furniture and gave them full credit against the new selection. The fully-upholstered furniture was far more expensive than the bamboo, and they happily paid the difference. As we waited for the new furniture, I did not ask for the balance due on the furniture we had removed. I also didn't ask for an increase in the deposit when they reselected. Yes, it went against the way we usually accept deposits, but in this instance it was the right thing to do. We were able to work with the supplier of the new furniture to speed up the delivery, and within five weeks the new selections were in place and both husband and wife were thrilled. Any losses with the original selection were more than made up for with the new, more expensive selection. The clients chose to request the new furniture, and our firm did not feel that we had pressured them into this decision. What, you ask, ultimately happened to the leather bamboo furniture? I actually ended up with furniture, which I use to this day, in my sunroom.

I realize not all discrepancies can be handled as easily, and often you will lose a little money, but by and large satisfying the client is the name of the game. At the very least, you should still maintain precise control over what is ordered and how it is delivered. Your profit depends on it. Also, do your best to ensure your client is completely satisfied. If you see or feel disappointment from your client during any delivery phase, ask about it right then and there. To wait is suicide. By addressing problems in the moment you will ensure that your clients are open with you about what they expect and will trust you to make adjustments as needed.

Clients are Family Members

Once a project concludes, the clients involved should be considered a group of satisfied clients. We never refer to them as "old," "past," or "finished." Considering them family, in the broadest sense of the term, is not presumptuous. And, as with all families, you want to stay in touch.

Photo postcards are a great way to stay in touch with all your clients and, when possible, I try to send the first card to the latest client family members within the first quarter of completion. I like the card to have a photograph of a room from their project. They find it exciting, inclusive, and special, and other "family" members get to see a newly completed project. Hopefully it will give them ideas for any new work they might need. If you aren't using a photo postcard system for contact you might include the project in your firm's newsletter, Web site, or blog.

Whatever you are using to keep in contact will ensure all of your clients are informed of developments within the firm and within the client family. Once a year you might consider throwing a party of some sort to include all your client family members. This way you get them together to talk amongst themselves, and, more importantly, to hear the latest news of the firm, told by you in the way you want them to hear it. This is a great way to maintain your word of mouth message–starting the word of mouth yourself and relaying it to your very best client family members. And, like all family, they will talk to each other. There is nothing as gratifying as listening to your client family tell one another how wonderful your designs are and how much they enjoy living in the space you created. Yes, it's okay to pat yourself on the back every once and a while.

The Post-Project Survey

I have found that one of the most beneficial tasks you can do after a completed project is conduct an exit or completion survey sent via e-mail. It should contain no more than eight or ten questions. Similar to the ongoing surveys discussed in chapter 6, this survey asks specific questions about performance, expectations, and successes. It also includes a question about whether or not the client would refer your firm to any other prospective clients. Don't be afraid to ask these questions. They are very important to the stability of your firm and the ongoing relationship you should have with past clients. The survey, like those in chapter 6, needs to be succinct and easy to complete. Your clients will be more inclined to send back the survey if they feel you are sincerely interested in a response. I would suggest including a short note from you or the lead designer, requesting their participation. It should be slightly personal and should explain how the information will be used within the firm to improve its performance on future projects.

Once the survey has been returned, you will look at the results and work with everyone involved in the project to ascertain what, if anything, should be done to improve the way you do business. This review should take place within two or three days of receipt of the survey, and a hand-written note should then be sent to the clients thanking them for their participation. You should emphasize how important their observations are to the success of your business and how the survey will continue to help the firm improve communication and outreach for all clients.

The survey need not, and should not, be overly long. You want the client to respond honestly and, if the survey is short enough, they will.

A Simple Exit Survey

1. How did you hear about Hale-Williams Interior Design?
2. What was your initial impression of our firm?

3. Were you happy with the initial meeting and is there anything you would have changed?

4. Did you interview other interior design firms?

5. Which firms did you interview, and why did you not select them?

6. What was your main reason for selecting Hale-Williams Interior Design?

7. Did you find our weekly surveys helpful in meeting your expectations?

8. What would you list as our greatest strength?

9. What do you believe is an area in need of improvement?

10. Would you use Hale-Williams Interior Design on future projects?

11. What do you think sets Hale-Williams Interior Design apart from other design firms?

12. Would you recommend us to other friends or colleagues?

We ask a total of twelve questions and most can be answered within one or two minutes. We request that they give us suggestions for areas in which we could improve as well as those areas in which the client found us to be particularly strong. Defining whether the clients would not only use you for their future projects but would also consider referrals to other potential clients is crucial. By making the clients a part of your team, they have a vested interest in your success. They will tell friends about the survey and will believe they are instrumental in your ability to manage projects and clients.

A Guarantee

From time to time you will find that clients will call with some problem or question about items you might have delivered some months if not years ago. You must make sure the question is addressed in a straightforward and timely manner. There will, of course, be some sort of guarantee from the manufacturer on most furniture items and built-ins. Working with them to take care of any problems that might arise should be relatively uncomplicated. Fabrics and wall coverings, however, present a unique set of problems. Most, if not all, fabrics will have been incorporated into furniture, drapery, bedspreads, or other decorative elements. If the fabric is in some way defective and the manufacturer takes responsibility for replacement, you must still consider the cost of remaking the item or items.

Particularly when working with fabrics and wallpaper, you must check before they are used that they are the correct item and color. You should also know how you are going to use the fabric in the space and whether or not it is suitable. Consider upholstery, for example. Most silks need to be knit-backed before application. Some cotton prints are too light-weight for seating and are better used for bedding and drapery. Here, again, it your responsibility to understand the products you are using and what the best choices are.

Biting the Bullet

If you discover, after working with the manufacturer, that the fabric is defective, arrange to have the item remade as soon as possible. Of course, you may not be able to use the same fabric. If it's defective the whole bolt may be unusable. Move on and make another selection. If, on the other hand, you discover you have used the fabric in an inappropriate way, simply take responsibility and make whatever adjustment is needed to satisfy the client. That might mean you will have to order new fabric, have it knit-backed, and use it to recover the piece in question, which is not an inexpensive undertaking. At this point, I have found many interior designers realize how important a markup, above the actual overhead expenses, is to making a profit and succeeding financially. The bottom line is, be sure you are educated about the correct and expected use of fabrics and furnishings you use. You are responsible for using the right item for the right piece. And, if you make a mistake, you must make it right.

If you and your team, including the manufacturer of any defective item, agree to replace or repair a piece, move forward as quickly as possible. Don't keep the clients hanging for weeks on end, waiting to get the item back. Clients will remember prompt responses to their queries and will respect your efficient and professional attitude. You may find the client has abused the item in question, in which case you should explain what happened and how it can be avoided. Clients with pets can be particularly troubling.

Claws and Furniture Don't Mix

Many years ago we delivered a beautiful set of custom-designed upholstered furniture, made locally and covered in a fine Brunschwig & Fils cotton print we had knit-backed to ensure stability. The furniture was delivered all at once and everything arrived in good order. The room was a wonderful realization of the clients wishes, and all of us were as pleased as we could be. The next morning, I received a telephone call from the client explaining they had found two very narrow slits on the arms of one of the lounge chairs. I went out immediately to inspect the problem and decide what to do. There were, indeed, two slits spaced about two inches apart on the left arm of the chair. I was at a loss to explain what could have happened. The only possibility I could come up with was that a razor knife had been used to open the wrap around the upholstered pieces during installation and somehow had damaged the arm. I arranged to have more fabric ordered and knit-baked, and worked with our local upholsterer to repair the arm on the chair. We inspected all the other furniture very closely with the client and found no other areas in which the same type of damage was apparent.

Forty-eight hours later I got another call from the client. The same type of slit had appeared on the arm of the sofa. She thought we must have missed these slits during our previous inspection. I assured her that we had not but went over to take a look. I arrived and we went into the room in question. As I stepped through the door her large cat leapt away and onto the arm of the sofa. His claws dug in as he missed and began to slide down the curve of the arm. We had found our culprit. The client was mortified and explained she never thought the cat could do that type of damage. We agreed to replace the fabric on the arms for her and they decided to try to keep the cat off the furniture. In this instance, I asked the client pay for the fabric and the cost of upholstery replacement, and we supplied the knit-backing at no charge to her. This was simply a way to convey to her that we understood how it could happen to anyone and we were happy to help.

Unexpected things can happen to any interior and your ability to respond in a professional manner and portray a heart-felt desire to help will keep your clients coming back. I often get questions, after the fact, about how to care for items. We have compiled a small, printed, three-fold brochure that explains how much of the fabric, wall covering, and flooring we supply should be cared for. Another strategy is to have cleaning services contact the client at some time after the delivery and installation to offer whatever type of cleaning is recommended for the particular pieces in the project. We include the cost of the first cleaning in the price of the item and maintain a file to ensure we follow-up when it is time to have the pieces cleaned. This helps the client understand how important maintenance is for the continued life and service of everything that went into the space.

When They Hire Another Designer

What should you do should the unthinkable happen and you discover your client has chosen another design professional to work on a project? First of all, ascertain the scope and location of the project and whether or not it is something you would have wanted to do. If the answer is yes, you might want to contact the client and offer to help in whatever way you can. Keep in mind, though, that at this point you don't want to be a nuisance. You can also let the client know you will be happy to contact the other design professional to offer any help he or she thinks your firm might be able to offer. I don't mean you will be trying to "horn in" on the design job; I simply mean that as a professional you are willing to offer assistance. There might be questions about previous fabric selections, seating composition, or paint choices. It's up to you to produce answers to those questions as quickly as possible and with as little fuss as possible. You shouldn't have to spend hours helping, and if the requests become too numerous and beyond the range of the previous project, you will have to explain to the client and other design professional how busy your firm is and that they might need to look to another source for that information. Don't ever be rude, but do be firm in your approach.

You might be upset with the client's choice to move to another design firm. You have every right to be. This is a time for you to take a look at why that client decided to move on. Even with exit surveys and constant contact, some clients will choose to use another design firm. If you can say honestly that you did everything you could to keep the client close, then you did your best. You also never know what might happen in the future. As they say, never burn a bridge behind you. You don't know when you might need it again.

Never Burn Bridges

We once worked with a client to complete a whole house renovation and continued to keep in contact. About eighteen months after the completion of the initial project, I heard from another designer that my client had signed with a firm in San Francisco to renovate an apartment she had recently bought there. Yes, I was surprised. Almost immediately the client called to ask about selections of fabrics we had made for the previous project. She explained that she was starting a new project with another design team and they wanted to look at what she had done before. I told her we would call back with the requested pattern numbers before the close of business that day and, with her permission, contact the other design team to offer any help they might need from our office. The design team never returned my telephone calls. I didn't hear from her for almost four weeks and thought she must have been well on her way to a completed design for the new condo. The next day she walked into my office without an appointment and in tears. Fortunately I wasn't working with another client and ushered her into my office. The whole awful story spilled out. She had gone with these designers because they were recommended by the realtor. She knew and trusted the realtor, and for a number of reasons hiring a new team seemed to be a good solution for her interior design needs.

Many realtors work with designers for referrals to purchasers, and we, too, have a list of realtors who refer us when out-of-town buyers come to Carmel. The new design team she selected was young, excited about the condo, and persuaded her they could create the space of her dreams within her budget. You know the rest. They wanted only to create what they felt was right for their particular interior design style and not what was right for the client. They would not listen to any of her thoughts and continued to override any attempt on her part to be involved in the process. Now she was in my office crying on my arm and wondering if I would work with her. She was under a deadline and needed a lot of decisions to be made very quickly. Of course we complied. We never spoke of the other design team, and her new project moved forward in a timely manner and with a minimum of complications. She explained months later that the only reason she even considered coming back to us was the very professional and prompt way in which we answered her request for fabric information when she decided to work with someone else. She said she knew we would respond to her current crisis in the same professional manner. I was glad to help and also glad I hadn't put her off when she called just because she chose to try another interior design firm.

It's on Record

In an age of instant communication, Internet technology, and wireless networking, it is interesting to note how much paper we continue to accumulate in our office. The vast majority tends to be past client files. We have considered numerous ways to reduce the size of these files, but some contain over five hundred different pieces of paper, and most offer a complete record of the projects. One of our concerns is that, over time, a lot of the items chosen for a particular project will become outdated. Fabrics are discontinued, furniture manufacturers delete items from their line, and building codes change and improve. With the amount of change that takes place, just how long should you maintain a client file? We have finally settled on six years. Yes, it is an arbitrary number and could just as easily be seven years.

The real point, of course, is to have a system in place for reducing the space taken up by past client files. We take one day a year and identify those client files that have been inactive for three years and compress the contents as much as possible, getting rid of items that are no longer useful. Each interior design firm will have its own criteria for which items to remove, and you will define what is right for your office. As you sort through these three-year-old files, you will come across items that no longer apply. Delete them and either shred them or recycle them as necessary. When you reach the six-year mark and are preparing to remove the file, you have a wonderful opportunity to contact your past clients.

Inform them that your office is preparing to remove their file from your records and ask if there is anything they feel might be important to have for their own records. It's possible they might want fabric or wall covering samples as well as tear sheets for furniture and accessory items used on the project. Mention these items as things they might possibly want for their personal files, and suggest they come into the office to pick up anything they would like to keep.

This will give you an opportunity to review what the past project was like and how exciting and productive the process was for all concerned. Do you see the possibilities? With luck they will become energized and excited about possibly working on a new project. Meeting to discuss the project again is certainly not a waste of time and allows you the chance to remind the client how accomplished you are at client and project management.

What Else Can You Do?

What other arrows do you have in your quiver of skills to keep clients a part of your firm? There are a number of things you can do beyond consistent mailing and inclusion in "family" gatherings. First and foremost, maintaining a professional presence in your area is vital. Continue to serve on community boards and to appear at local meetings and mixers. If you teach, keep offering your services to whatever institution you are most comfortable with. Every so often be sure to host an in-house seminar or trunk show to attract the public at large to listen to your ideas on interior design and home furnishings.

Everyone with whom you have ever worked needs to be able to reach you easily. That means keeping your business address the same, if at all possible. If you do decide to move, for whatever reason, proper communication is important in letting everyone know that you've moved your office and why. Tell the story in a newspaper or magazine ad. If you can, have a feature article written about the move. You can put whatever spin you want on the piece. You might tell everyone you became so busy that a larger space was needed. Or a smaller space was desirable to enable you to reorganize and save space. You might also tell everyone you simply wanted to be nearer to your client base. The reason doesn't really matter, just be sure it makes sense to you and your clients. Don't change your telephone number every few years and make sure you consistently include updates in the local newspaper. Just because you don't have it delivered anymore doesn't mean your older and wealthier clients don't. As a matter of fact, most clients over fifty still read a daily newspaper. Not all are online.

The second thing you should do is perfect your ability to speak in public and tell your story to anyone who will listen. I once knew a very successful and accomplished interior designer in Baltimore, Maryland, whose work I thought was superior to mine and of whom I was envious. Not a nice thing to be sure, but there you have it. I had been appearing live on a local television network every other Saturday morning for about eight weeks. For the first five minutes I would talk about a specific subject in interior design. I would then answer questions for another ten minutes from viewers watching the show. I found it all a lot of fun and wasn't intimidated by appearing live on television. My interior designer friend told me he just couldn't easily do what he saw me doing and asked what made it easy for me. Being featured on TV is, for me, as simple as having a broad knowledge of my subject and a willingness to share with anyone who will listen. That's why I teach and why I speak whenever given the opportunity. My designer friend asked me to help him master the art and I asked him to show me more of his designs. We each saw in the other something we felt we lacked. It cemented the friendship in a way nothing else could have and we shared lots of thoughts about a variety of subjects over the next few years. I learned a tremendous amount about how he organized his business and he learned a lot about being more comfortable in public. This was a wonderful way to share talents and improve the playing field for both.

I have tried, over the years, to make friends with local designers in whatever part of the world I live. I don't try to elicit their secrets of the trade, but I do share stories from the trenches. It might sound silly, but learning what other designers are going through with clients and staff and showrooms and reps helps me to become more centered on what I do with my own business. I share information about my own experiences and hear how other designers handle the challenges of day-to-day business. First as a sole proprietor, later as a corporate entity, and, finally, today as a partner in a boutique firm, I find the interaction between professionals interesting and very helpful. Reach out to your fellow designers, and you just might discover a soul mate in a designer's clothing. All designers, after all, are running businesses and trying to juggle all the different facets of the industry.

Is There a Secret?

Have you figured it all out, yet? Do you know all the answers? If so, give me a call. I could use the help. There are always going to be new and innovative ways to acquire, serve, and maintain a diverse and interesting clientele. How you use the tools available and create new ones will speak volumes about your skills as a client and project manager. It's possible that the Internet and social networking sites have just scratched the surface of how this new type of marketing can help your business succeed. Whether it's a blog or a tweet, what you send out on the Web could bring you increased attention from prospective and current clients. As we become more adept at utilizing these new tools we'll also discover new ways to send our messages out. Will everyone hear them? No, but if handled properly you can get your specific message to your specific prospective clientele through any medium you choose.

As clients come to you for the first time or the seventh your ability to manage how the project unfolds will continue to be what this business is all about. These tools and others will help you maintain an open line of communication with each and every prospective and current client. The better your office is at using all or part of the package of client and project management tools, the better your clientele will be. I promise.

AFTERWORD

Over the past thirty-five years I have owned and managed several different firms, pursued various business objectives and used an array of tax entities to achieve our goals. My firms and I have been fortunate over the years to work with clients on projects in different parts of the world. We created interiors for a sprawling historic farmhouse in Maryland, a beautiful five-story townhouse on the Upper East Side of Manhattan, and a stunning Spanish Colonial residence in Los Angeles for the same client over a period of about five years. We loved the scope and diversity of the projects and the client liked the way we did business. Most of our clients also understood we weren't glued to one particular style of interior design and appreciated our ability to work on historic projects while maintaining a current and modern approach to the design process. We developed a wonderful working relationship and understood one another's needs. With projects in Scotland, Chicago, Philadelphia, London, and many other parts of the United States, we were able to grow with the scope of our projects. Not all were large and many were done on a very small budget. As so often happens we did, indeed, work on more than one project for the same client in different cities.

The fact that some of these projects were in different cities doesn't matter as much as the fact that our clients decided to trust us with the projects. When I created my first solo firm in 1978, I created processes that would work for a sole proprietor as well as a corporation. Client and project management is all about sustainable systems that allow the work to flow smoothly and efficiently. In the beginning it was time consuming to create the proper system. At times I felt overwhelmed by process minutia. In the end, the systems became part of the process and I increased the size of my staff to facilitate what needed to be done. By the time my firm was large enough to actually become a corporate entity, most of the systems were in place, creating a seamless transition. I encourage all interior designers, whether experienced or new to the field, to install processes and systems that will sustain them for the long haul. To be successful in this industry, a sound business footing is essential. Systems and processes help maintain that solid grounding and keep your clients and projects in line, on time, and on budget. Acquiring and keeping a qualified clientele should be part of your overall business strategy and included in any business plan you might develop.

Defining your optimum clients and understanding how best to reach out to them is the first step. A contract or letter of agreement that explains precisely what is expected from all parties ensures the project will move forward with a minimum of fuss. Good communication, preparation, and presentation skills enhance your ability to manage and maintain your best clients and will pave the way for stress-free procurement and delivery of all items ordered. Finally, you will have many of these clients coming back to you, year after year, for the new projects they will undoubtedly develop.

With this, my second book, and my first book, *Starting Your Career as an Interior Designer,* I have attempted to empower each and every reader to succeed in the highly competitive world of professional interior design. It is my belief that everyone who wants to pursue a career as an interior designer should be first and foremost aware of the business acumen required to succeed. It is, after all, the *business* of interior design. Those coming to the field with the belief that all one needs to prevail is exceedingly good taste are in for quite a shock. Those of you prepared to study the basics of good business, the process of client and project management, and the intricacies of a successful sales technique will be successful in our complex and exciting business.

The best time to get into the business of interior design is the present. How do I know? No matter what the economic condition, starting your own business is a risk only a few will even contemplate. You already have an edge over most of the other poor souls out there who don't know where to begin. You also now have the knowledge, and the power, to create a highly successful and exciting business. Will you have problems along the way? Yes. Will you surmount those challenges and continue to move your business and your designs into the future? Yes. With tenacity and an unfaltering belief in your ability to manage your business and your clients, your success as an entrepreneurial interior designer is assured.

Good luck.

INDEX

Books from Allworth Press

Allworth Press is an imprint of Allworth Communications, Inc. Selected titles are listed below.

Starting Your Career as an Interior Designer
by Robert K. Hale and Thomas L. Williams (6 × 9, 240 pages, paperback, $24.95)

Marketing Interior Design
by Lloyd Princeton (6 × 9, 224 pages, paperback, $24.95)

Interior Design Practice
by Cindy Coleman (6 × 9, 256 pages, paperback, $24.95)

The Interior Designer's Guide to Pricing, Estimating, and Budgeting, Second Edition
by Theo Stephan Williams (6 × 9, 208 pages, paperback, $24.95)

How to Start and Operate Your Own Design Firm: A Guide for Interior Designers and Architects
by Albert W. Rubeling (6 × 9, 256 pages, paperback, $24.95)

Business and Legal Forms for Interior Designers
by Tad Crawford and Eva Doman Bruck (8 ½ × 11, 208 pages, paperback, $29.95)

Green Interior Design
by Lori Dennis (8 ½ × 10, 144 pages, paperback, $24.95)

How to Start a Faux Painting or Mural Business, Second Edition
by Rebecca Pittman (6 × 9, 256 pages, $24.95)

The Challenge of Interior Design: Professional Values and Opportunities
by Mary V. Knackstedt (6 × 9, 272 pages, paperback, $24.95)

To request a free catalog or order books by credit card, call 1-800-491-2808. To see our complete catalog on the World Wide Web, or to order online, please visit ***www.allworth.com***.